THE WAY OF
A PILGRIM

THE WAY OF
A PILGRIM

TRANSLATED FROM THE RUSSIAN BY
OLGA SAVIN

FOREWORD BY
FATHER THOMAS HOPKO

SHAMBHALA
Boston & London
1996

Shambhala Publications, Inc.
Horticultural Hall
300 Massachusetts Avenue
Boston, Massachusetts 02115

9 8 7 6 5 4 3 2 1

FIRST EDITION

Printed in Canada

♻ This edition is printed on acid-free paper that meets
the American National Standards Institute Z39.48 Standard.

Distributed in the United States by Random House, Inc.,
and in Canada by Random House of Canada Ltd.

Library of Congress Cataloging-in-Publication Data

Otkrovennye rasskazy strannika dukhovnomu svoemu ott͡su. English.
The way of a pilgrim/translated by Olga Savin.
p.   cm.
ISBN 1-57062-201-9 (alk. paper)
1. Jesus prayer.   2. Spiritual life—Orthodox Eastern Church.
3. Orthodox Eastern Church—Doctrines.   I. Savin, Olga.   II. Title.
BX382.O8513   1996   95-38770
248.4′819—dc20   CIP

CONTENTS

FOREWORD

THE ORIGIN OF this little spiritual classic is in many ways a mystery. No one knows for certain if it is a literally true story written by the narrator, or an account cast in the first person *about* a particular pilgrim (or perhaps based on several), or even a marvelously creative piece of spiritual fiction intended to propagate a certain understanding of the practice of the Orthodox Christian faith, and the prayer of the heart, particularly the Jesus prayer.

Whatever the origin and intention of the anonymous author's fascinating story, *The Way of a Pilgrim* makes several things clear to spiritual seekers. It affirms first of all that the source, goal and content of human life is not spirituality or religion, liturgical ritual or ascetical regimes, but the living God Himself. It tells us that life is communion with God: personal, direct, immediate, real, painful, peaceful, and joyful. It tells us that ceaseless prayer in pursuit of God and communion with Him is not simply life's meaning or goal, the one thing worth living for, but it is life itself. It tells us that Jesus Christ is this life, and that constant, continual, ceaseless prayer in His name opens the door to Divine reality and puts us in immediate contact with the One who is the source, substance, and goal of our life, and our very life itself.

The pilgrim learns these things in the context of the Orthodox Church. His inspiration comes in the liturgical worship which he faithfully follows and never abandons, and through the Bible, which he constantly carries with him as his greatest treasure. He searches for someone to help him to understand prayer and to practice it without ceasing. He finds people and writings that help him, often in the most unexpected places. He discovers the collection of writings of Christian spiritual masters, mostly Eastern and all Orthodox, called the *Philokalia* (which literally means love of the good and beautiful), with his whole life testifying to its teachings with disarming directness and awesome simplicity. What does he say about its message and teaching?

He says that one cannot practice ceaseless prayer in the name of Jesus outside the doctrinal and liturgical framework of the Christian Church and without the guidance and help of experienced teachers. He says that attempts to do this will be futile and fruitless and will inevitably lead to the spiritual delusion that is the perpetual risk of the spiritual seeker. While insisting on personal responsibility in the spiritual quest and on the radically personal character of prayer, the pilgrim insists equally on the need for participation in the community of faith with free and grateful obedience to its teachers and guides. He stresses the confession of sins and the need for perpetual repentance and moral conversion.

The pilgrim also stresses that the practice of prayer, which is the "art of arts" and "science of sciences" that proves everything else in a person's life, is a ceaseless labor whose fruit is always the result of God's grace. It is a disinterested activity—characterized by an interest only in God's glory and the salvation of souls, first of all one's own. It provokes the demons to relentless and ruthless attack. It invites the ridicule and rejection of the world. It excites the passions of mind and flesh before it cures their misuse and heals their abuse, and directs them to their proper end. It is practiced not to gain extraordinary experiences or unique consolations. It teaches us to fear visions and voices and every such thing as the source of great temptation, confusion, and pain. It is always accompanied by the peace which passes understanding and the joy which no one can take away, yet it inevitably involves suffering, of which the pilgrim is the first witness. For the purpose of ceaseless prayer is not to remove the crosses of pain and difficulty, but to empower the praying person to endure them and even to embrace them with enthusiasm and joy as the sole source of happiness in this sad sinful world in which we find ourselves wandering as pilgrims in pursuit of our homeland.

The pilgrim also tells us that the constant repetition of the Jesus prayer, or any other such prayer of the heart, is not a magical or mechanical means to spiritual peace and perfection. The prayer is not an incantation or a talisman. It is a *prayer*: a personal calling upon the personal God. It is a petition for the Lord to act as He knows and wills for our purification, enlightenment, and deification in an unending life of growth and perfection.

The Way of a Pilgrim reminds us that we are all pilgrims on a journey to God. Like a safe and hospitable inn along the way, this little book provides protection and nourishment for the trip, pointing to its perils and demonstrating its rewards. We greet Olga Savin's fresh new translation with gratitude and joy.

FATHER THOMAS HOPKO
Saint Vladimir's Seminary,
Crestwood, New York

THE WAY OF
A PILGRIM

FIRST
NARRATIVE

B Y THE GRACE OF GOD I am a Christian man, by my own actions a great sinner, and by calling a homeless wanderer of the humblest origins, roaming from place to place. My worldly belongings consist of a knapsack on my back, containing some dried bread, and a Holy Bible in my breast pocket. That is all.

On the twenty-fourth Sunday after Pentecost I went to church to worship at the Liturgy. During the reading of the Epistle of Saint Paul to the Thessalonians [1 Thess. 5:17] I heard the following words: "Pray without ceasing." This verse especially fixed itself in my mind, and I began to wonder how one could pray unceasingly, since each man must occupy himself with other matters as well, in order to make a living. I checked in the Bible and read with my own eyes that which I had already heard: namely, that one should "pray without ceasing," "pray at all times in the Spirit" [Ephes. 6:18], and "in all places pray with uplifted hands" [1 Tim. 2:8]. I thought about this for some time but was unable to understand it.

"What should I do?" I thought to myself. "Where will I find someone who would be able to explain this to me? I will visit some of the churches that are renowned for their excellent preachers, and perhaps there I will be enlightened." So I went and I heard many fine sermons on prayer. However, they all dealt with prayer in general: what prayer is, the need to pray, and what are the fruits of prayer. Yet nothing was said about how to succeed in prayer. There was a sermon on praying in the Spirit and on unceasing prayer, but no mention was made about how to attain to such prayer.

Having had my fill of listening, without acquiring any understanding of how to pray unceasingly, I gave up on such sermons that were geared to the general public. I then resolved, with the help of God, to seek an experienced and knowledgeable guide who would explain unceasing prayer to me, for I now found myself so irresistibly drawn to learning about it.

I set out and wandered for a long time through different places and faithfully continued to read the Bible. Everywhere I went I inquired as to the local whereabouts of a spiritual director or a devout spiritual guide. Eventually I was told that in a certain village there was a landowner who had lived there for a long time and who spent all his time working out his salvation. He had a chapel in his own house and never went out, but continually prayed to God and read spiritual literature. When I heard this I gave up walking and took to my heels to get to this village. When I arrived there, I found the gentleman in question. "What is it that you require of me?" he asked.

"I have heard that you are a man of prayer and wisdom. In the name of God, would you please explain to me the meaning of the Apostle's words, 'Pray unceasingly,' and how one is to pray in this manner? I want to know this, yet I cannot understand it at all!"

He was silent for some moments. Then he looked closely at me and said, "Unceasing interior prayer is the continual striving of man's spirit toward God. To succeed in this delightful exercise, you must beseech the Lord more frequently that He teach you how to pray unceasingly. Pray more and ever more earnestly, and the prayer itself will reveal to you how it can become unceasing. This effort will take its own time."

Having said this, he offered me refreshment, gave me money for my journey, and let me go on my way. He did not, after all, provide me with an explanation.

So I set off again. I continued to think and read and wonder about what that man had told me, and still I could not understand it. Yet my longing for comprehension was so intense that it kept me awake at night.

When I had covered about 125 miles I came to a large provincial capital, where I saw a monastery. I stopped at the inn and happened to hear that in this monastery there was an exceptionally kind abbot, a prayerful and most hospitable man. I went to see him, and he welcomed me joyfully, sat me down, and offered me refreshment.

"Holy Father," I said, "I do not need food, but I seek your spiritual guidance on what I must do to save myself."

"Well, now—what must you do to save yourself? Live according to the commandments, pray to God—and you will be saved!"

"I have heard that one should pray unceasingly, but I do not know how to do this. I do not even understand what unceasing prayer is. My father, please explain this to me."

"I don't know, dear brother, how else to advise you. Ah—but wait just a moment! I do have a little book that will explain it." He brought me *The Spiritual Education of the Interior Man*, by Saint Dimitri. "Here you are—read this page."

I began to read the following: "Those words of the apostle—'pray without ceasing'—should be understood in reference to the prayer of the mind: for the mind can always aspire to God and pray to Him without ceasing."

"Would you explain to me the means by which the mind can always aspire to God and pray unceasingly, without being distracted?"

"That requires a great deal of wisdom, except for

the one to whom God Himself has granted such a gift,"
said the abbot. He offered no further explanation.

I spent the night at the monastery. The next morning I thanked him for his kind hospitality and continued on my journey, without really knowing where I
was headed. I grieved over my lack of understanding
and comforted myself by reading the Holy Bible. Thus
I journeyed for five days, keeping to the main road.
Finally, one day toward evening, an old man who appeared to be some kind of cleric caught up with me.
In answer to my question, he replied that he was a
schima monk* and lived in a monastery, located some
six miles off the main road. He invited me to come
with him, to visit their monastery. "We take in pilgrims," said he, "and we offer them rest and food in
the guesthouse, along with other devout people."

I was reluctant to go with him, so I replied, "My
peace of mind does not depend on finding shelter, but
rather on obtaining spiritual guidance. I do not need
food, for my knapsack is filled with dried crusts of
bread."

The monk asked, "What sort of guidance do you
seek, and what is it that you do not understand? Come,
dear brother, come and visit with us. We have experi-

---

*Words marked with an asterisk in their first occurrence are found in
the glossary.

enced *startsi** who can nourish you spiritually and set you on the path of truth, in the light of God's Word and the teachings of the Fathers."

"Well, you see, Batyushka,* about a year ago, while at Liturgy, I heard the words of the apostle, exhorting men to 'pray unceasingly.' Unable to understand this, I began to read the Bible. There, in several different places, I also encountered this same divine instruction: that we must pray unceasingly, always and in all places, not only while occupied with all manner of activity, not only when we are awake, but even while we sleep. 'I sleep but my heart is awake' [Song of Songs 5:2]. This surprised me, and I found myself unable to understand how this could be done and by what means it could be achieved. A burning desire and curiosity were aroused in me, and my thoughts dwelt on it day and night. So I began to visit many different churches and to listen to sermons that spoke about prayer. Yet no matter how many sermons I heard, not one of them provided me with an explanation of how to pray unceasingly. They spoke only of how to prepare oneself for praying, of the fruits of prayer, and so on; but they did not teach how one is to pray unceasingly and what is the nature of this sort of prayer. I frequently read the Bible to verify what I had heard, but I have not yet found the knowledge I seek. I am not at peace with myself and am still quite puzzled by all this."

The starets made the sign of the cross over himself and began to speak: "Thank God, beloved brother, for having awakened in you this irresistible longing to acquire unceasing interior prayer. You must recognize in this the calling of God. Be at peace and rest assured that until now you have been tested in the cooperation of your will with God's calling and have been granted to understand that neither the wisdom of this world nor mere superficial curiosity can attain to the divine illumination of unceasing interior prayer. On the contrary, it is the humble, simple heart that attains to such prayer, through poverty of the spirit and a living experience of it. So it is not at all surprising that you heard nothing about the very essence of prayer nor acquired any knowledge on how to achieve its unceasing activity.

"To tell the truth, although much has been preached on prayer and much is written about it in the teaching of various writers, they are better equipped to preach about the elements that constitute prayer than about the very essence of it, because their thoughts are based mostly on speculation and the deliberations of natural reason, rather than on a living experience of prayer. One will offer an exceptional discourse on the necessity of prayer, another on its power and benefits; yet a third will discuss the means to attaining to perfect prayer—the necessity of applied effort, attentiveness, warmth of heart, purity of thought, reconciliation with one's enemies, humility, contrition, and so on. But what about prayer itself, and how to learn to pray? To these, the most essential and necessary questions of all, very rarely does one obtain any substantial answers from present-day preachers. Such questions are far more difficult for their understanding to grasp than are all those arguments of theirs that I just mentioned, for they require a mystical insight that goes above and beyond mere academic knowledge. And what is even more pathetic is that the vain, natural wisdom of this world compels one to judge the Divine according to human standards. Many people treat prayer in an inverted way, thinking that it is one's efforts and the preparatory steps that give rise to prayer, rather than the prayer itself giving birth to good works and all the virtues. In this case, they mistakenly see the fruits and resulting benefits of prayer as the means to its end, thereby denigrating the very power of prayer.

"All this stands in direct contradiction to Holy Scripture, for the apostle Paul teaches us the following about prayer: 'I urge therefore that first of all supplications . . . be made . . .' [1 Tim. 2:1]. Here we see that the apostle's first emphasis is on the preeminence of the activity of prayer: 'I urge therefore that first of all supplications . . . be made. . . .' Many good works are required of a Christian, but it is prayer that must come first and foremost, for without prayer no other good work can be performed and one cannot find the way to the Lord. Truth cannot be acquired, the flesh with its passions and lusts cannot be crucified, the heart cannot be filled with the light of Christ and united with Him, through salvation, unless these are preceded by frequent prayer. I say *frequent*, because the proper way to pray and to attain to perfect prayer lies beyond our abilities. The apostle Paul says: 'For we do not know how to pray as we ought' [Rom. 8:26]. Consequently, it is only the frequency and regularity of prayer that lie within our abilities, as the means of attaining to pure prayer, which is the mother of all spiritual blessings. 'Acquire the mother and she will bear you children,' says Saint Isaac the Syrian. First learn to pray, and then you will easily perform all the good works. This is not obvious to those who lack a living experience of prayer and the knowledge of the mystical teachings of the Fathers, so they say very little about it."

So engrossed were we in this conversation that without realizing it, we had almost reached the monastery. Not wanting to lose touch with this wise starets and eager to obtain what I desired from him, I quickly said, "Would you be so kind, honorable Father, to explain to me the meaning of unceasing interior prayer and how one can learn it? I can see that you have experience of it and know it well."

The starets lovingly acknowledged my request and

invited me to come with him. "Come inside with me now, and I will give you a book of the writings of the Fathers from which, with God's help, you will be able to learn and understand about prayer, clearly and in detail." We entered his cell, and the starets said the following to me: "The unceasing interior Jesus prayer is the uninterrupted, continual calling upon the divine name of Jesus Christ, with the lips, the mind, and the heart, while calling to mind His constant presence and beseeching His mercy, during any activity one may be occupied with, in all places, at all times, and even while sleeping. The words of this prayer are as follows: 'Lord Jesus Christ, have mercy on me!' If one makes a habit of this supplication, one will experience great comfort and a need to repeat this prayer unceasingly, so that eventually one will not be able to live without it and the prayer will flow of its own accord.

"Now is it clear to you what unceasing prayer is?"

"Very clear, my Father! For God's sake, teach me how to acquire it," I cried out with joy.

"We can read about how to learn the prayer in this book, whose title is the *Philokalia.** It contains the complete and detailed teaching on unceasing interior prayer, as set forth by twenty-five holy Fathers. It is so lofty in wisdom and so beneficial that it is considered to be the foremost and primary manual of the contemplative spiritual life. The blessed Nikifor said that 'without struggle and sweat does it bring one to salvation.' "

"Is it possible that it is more exalted and holier than the Bible?" I asked.

"No, it is not more exalted or holier than the Bible, but it contains enlightened explanations of what is mystically contained in the Bible and is so lofty that it is not easily comprehended by our shortsighted intellects. Let me give you an example of this: the sun is the greatest, the most resplendent and magnificent source of light; but you cannot contemplate or examine it with the simple naked eye. You would need to use a special viewing lens, which, albeit a million times smaller and dimmer than the sun, would enable you to study this magnificent lord of all light and to endure and delight in its fiery rays. Thus the Holy Scriptures are like a brilliant sun, for which the *Philokalia* is the necessary viewing lens.

"Now listen, I will read to you about how to learn unceasing interior prayer." The starets opened the *Philokalia*, selected a passage from Saint Simeon the New Theologian, and began to read: " 'Find a quiet place to sit alone and in silence; bow your head and shut your eyes. Breathe softly, look with your mind into your heart; recollect your mind—that is, all its thoughts—and bring them down from your mind into your heart. As you breathe, repeat: "Lord Jesus Christ, have mercy on me"—either quietly with your lips, or only in your mind. Strive to banish all thoughts; be calm and patient, and repeat this exercise frequently.' "

Then the starets explained all this to me, illustrated it with examples, and we read some more from the *Philokalia*: passages from Saint Gregory of Sinai, the blessed Callistus and Ignatius. After reading all this in the *Philokalia*, the starets further explained it to me in his own words. I was fascinated and listened attentively to every word he said, absorbing it with my mind in as much detail as I was capable of remembering. Thus we spent the entire night, without sleeping a wink, and then went off to matins.

When we were parting, the starets blessed me and said that while learning the prayer, I should come to see him and reveal and confess all to him honestly and openly, for it is difficult and futile to live an inner spiritual life properly, without the guidance of a spiritual director.

Standing in church, I experienced a burning zeal within me to learn unceasing interior prayer as diligently as possible, and I asked God to help me in this effort. Then I thought to myself: how will I visit the starets for counsel and confession, when the monastery guesthouse has a three-day limit for visitors and there are no other residences near the monastery?

Finally I happened to hear that there was a village a little over three miles away. I went there in search of a place to stay and was overjoyed that God had led me to find lodging. A peasant hired me to guard his kitchen garden for the entire summer, in exchange for which I could live alone in a hut near the garden. Thank God! I had found peaceful lodging. So I settled into my dwelling and began to learn interior prayer according to the way I'd been taught, and I visited the starets from time to time.

For a week, in the seclusion of the garden, I worked diligently on learning unceasing prayer and I did what the starets had taught me. At first it seemed as if things were moving along. Then a great inner heaviness, laziness, boredom, and drowsiness began to overcome me, while a mass of thoughts clouded my mind. Filled with grief, I went to see the starets and explained my problems to him. He greeted me kindly and said, "That, beloved brother, is the kingdom of darkness waging war against you. There is nothing more dreadful for this darkness than the prayer of the heart, so it will try anything to thwart you and prevent you from learning to pray. Come to think of it, even the enemy can act only by God's will and permission, and only for as long as it may be necessary for us. It appears that your humility still needs to be tested. Consequently, it is too soon for you to be attempting to enter into your deepest heart with such unrestrained zeal, lest you succumb to spiritual avarice. I will read to you what the *Philokalia* says about this."

The starets found a passage from the teaching of Blessed Nicephorus the Solitary and began to read: " 'If, after a few attempts, you are unable to enter into the place of the heart, as you were taught to do, then do what I tell you and, with God's help, you will find what you seek. You know that each person has a larynx through which he exercises his faculty of speech. Banishing all thoughts (you can do this, if you want to), exercise this faculty and continually repeat the following: "Lord Jesus Christ, have mercy on me!" Compel yourself always to repeat this. Should you do this for some period of time, then assuredly this exercise will open the doors of your heart. Experience has proven this.'

"So this is what the holy Fathers prescribe in such cases," said the starets. "Therefore, you must accept this teaching now with complete trust and repeat the Jesus prayer as often as possible. Take this *chotki** and use it while you repeat the prayer, at least three thousand times a day to begin with. Whether you are standing, sitting, walking, or lying down, continue to repeat: 'Lord Jesus Christ, have mercy on me!' Do not be loud or rush the prayer, but without fail repeat it three thousand times each day, neither increasing nor decreasing this number on your own. Through this exercise God will help you to attain to the unceasing prayer of the heart."

I joyfully accepted his instructions, went home, and began to carry out the bidding of the starets faithfully and accurately. For two days I experienced some difficulty, but then the exercise became so easy and so desirable that if I stopped, I experienced a kind of compelling need to start reciting the Jesus prayer again. Soon I was praying it with comfort and ease, without any of the force that I initially had to exert.

I related this to the starets, who instructed me to increase the number of repetitions to six thousand times a day. "Be calm and just try to repeat the prayer as faithfully as you can, for the number of times I have assigned to you. God will bestow His mercy on you."

For an entire week, in the solitude of my hut, I repeated the Jesus prayer six thousand times a day. I was not anxious about anything and paid no heed to any thoughts, no matter how strongly they assailed me. I concentrated only on precisely carrying out the starets's instructions. And do you know what happened? I became so accustomed to the prayer that when I stopped praying, even for a brief time, I felt as though something were missing, as if I had lost something. When I began to pray again, I was immediately filled with an inner lightness and joy. If I happened to meet people, I no longer felt any desire to speak with them; I longed only for solitude, to be alone with my prayer.

Thus it was that within a week I had become so accustomed to this prayer.

After ten days of not seeing me, the starets himself came to visit me, and I described my inner state to him. He listened and said, "Now that you have become accustomed to the prayer, take care to preserve and strengthen this habit. Do not pass your time in vain and, with God's help, resolve to repeat the prayer, without fail, twelve thousand times a day. Remain in solitude, rise earlier in the morning, retire later at night, and come to me for counsel every two weeks."

I began to carry out the starets's instructions. By late evening of the first day, I had barely managed to complete the rule of twelve thousand repetitions of the prayer. On the second day, I fulfilled the rule with ease and delight. At first I was weary from continuously repeating the prayer. My tongue became numb and my jaws felt stiff, although the sensations were not unpleasant. I then felt a subtle, delicate pain in the roof of my mouth, followed by a slight pain in the thumb of my left hand, with which I was counting the knots of the chotki. My left wrist felt inflamed, and this feeling spread up to my elbow, creating a most pleasant sensation. Moreover, all this was somehow urging and compelling me to pray more and more. Thus for the first five days I faithfully repeated the prayer twelve thousand times a day. As this habit became stronger, it also became more pleasant and I found myself more willing to practice it.

Early one morning somehow the prayer awakened me. I began to recite my morning prayers, but my tongue was reluctant to say them, while all my desire seemed to be striving, as if with a mind of its own, toward reciting the Jesus prayer. As soon as I began to repeat it, I was filled with such lightness and joy that it felt as if my tongue and mouth spoke the words of their own accord, without any effort on my part! I spent the entire day enveloped in such joy and somehow detached from everything else—almost as if I were on another planet. By early evening I had easily completed the twelve thousand repetitions of the prayer. I had a strong desire to continue praying, but I dared not exceed the rule given to me by the starets. In the days that followed, I continued to call on the name of Jesus Christ with such ease and feeling so drawn to it.

Then I visited the starets and honestly recounted all this to him in detail. He listened and said, "Thank God that the ease and desire for prayer have been manifested in you. This is a natural consequence that comes from frequent practice and great effort. It is similar to a piece of equipment that can operate for a long time on its own, once its main drive has been activated; but in order for it to continue operating, the drive must be oiled and regularly reactivated. Now do you see with what superior abilities God, in His love for man, has endowed even the most sensual human nature—and what feelings can be experienced even outside a state of grace, even by a sinful soul with unclean passions, as you yourself have already experienced? Yet how magnificent, how delightful and enjoyable it is when the Lord bestows the gift of unceasing self-acting prayer and purifies the soul of its passions! This state is indescribable, and the revelation of the mystery of such prayer is a foretaste of heavenly bliss on earth. This is granted to those who seek the Lord in the simplicity of a heart filled with love! I now give you leave to repeat the prayer as much as you desire and as frequently as possible. Strive to devote every waking moment to prayer. Do not count the number of repetitions anymore, but call on the name of Jesus Christ, submitting yourself humbly to the will of God and awaiting His help. I believe that He will not abandon you and will set you on the right path."

Accepting this guidance, I spent the entire summer continuously repeating the Jesus prayer with my lips. I was very much at peace and often even dreamed that I was uttering this prayer. If I happened to meet people during the day, without exception they all appeared very dear to me, as if they were family, though otherwise I did not concern myself too much with them. All thoughts seemed to vanish on their own, and I thought of nothing else but the prayer. My mind was

The Way of a Pilgrim

recollected and attentive to it, while at times and of its own accord, my heart would feel a warmth and a kind of pleasure. When I happened to go to church, the long monastic service would seem so short and was no longer as tiring as it once had been for me. My solitary hut seemed like a magnificent palace, and I knew not how to thank God for sending such a starets and guide for the salvation of a wretched sinner such as I.

It was not for long that I enjoyed the counsel of my kind, divinely inspired starets, however, for at the end of that summer he died. As I tearfully parted with him, I thanked him for the fatherly counsel he had given to wretched me and begged him to give me, for a blessing and keepsake, the chotki he always used to pray with. And so I was left all alone. The summer finally drew to an end, and the kitchen garden was cleared. I was left with nowhere to live. The peasant released me from my job, paying me a wage of two rubles, and filled my knapsack with dried bread for my journey. Once again I set off wandering through different places, but now my travels were free of worry. Calling on the name of Jesus Christ now filled my days with joy. Each person I encountered seemed dearer to me, as if all were filled with love for me.

At one point I began to wonder what to do with the wages I'd earned for guarding the kitchen garden. What did I need money for? "Aha!" I thought, "I've got it! The starets is no longer around and there is no one to teach me. So I'll buy myself a copy of the *Philokalia* and continue learning about interior prayer." I made the sign of the cross over myself and went on walking and praying. When I came to a provincial town, I searched through the shops for a copy of the *Philokalia*. I found one, but they were asking three rubles for it, while I had only two! After I had bargained for a long time, the shopkeeper still refused to lower the price. Finally he said, "Go to that church over there and ask the parish elder. He has an old copy of this book; maybe he'll sell it to you for two rubles." I went there and actually managed to buy the *Philokalia* for two rubles! It was an old, worn copy, but I was thrilled. I managed to mend it somewhat by covering it with a piece of fabric, and I placed it in my knapsack, together with my Bible.

I set out again, continuously praying the Jesus prayer, which had become more precious and sweeter to me than anything else in the world. There were days when I covered forty-seven miles or more, and I didn't even feel the effort of walking. The prayer alone filled my consciousness. When it was bitterly cold, I would pray more fervently, and soon I'd feel warm all over. If hunger threatened to overcome me, I would call upon the name of Jesus Christ with renewed vigor, and soon my hunger was forgotten. If I felt ill and pain racked my back and legs, I would give myself over to the prayer and soon was deaf to the pain. If someone offended me, I needed only to remember the sweetness of the Jesus prayer, and all hurt and anger vanished, all was forgotten. It was as if I'd become a half-wit, for I had no cares about anything, nothing interested me. I cared not for the vain concerns of this world and longed only for solitude. I was now used to desiring only one thing: to pray unceasingly, for that filled me with joy. God alone knows what was happening to me! Yet of course, all these feelings were sensual, or, as my late starets would say, a natural consequence of habit. However, in my unworthiness and foolishness, I dared not venture yet to learn and aspire to the prayer of the inner heart. I awaited the fulfillment of God's will, setting my hopes on the prayers of my departed starets. And so, though I had not yet achieved the unceasing self-acting prayer of the heart, still I thanked God! For now I understood clearly the meaning of the apostle's words that I had heard: "Pray without ceasing!"

SECOND
NARRATIVE

FOR A LONG TIME I wandered through different places accompanied by the Jesus prayer, which encouraged and comforted me wherever I went, no matter what or whom I encountered. Finally, I began to think it might be better for me to settle down somewhere, so as to find enough time and solitude to study the *Philokalia*. Although I had managed to read bits of it whenever I stopped for the night or to rest during the day, I dearly longed to immerse myself in it without interruption and, with faith, to learn from it the true way to salvation through the prayer of the heart.

However, despite my wishes and because of the disability I'd had in my left arm from early childhood, I could not find any suitable work. Since I was unable to manage the upkeep of a permanent residence, I headed for Siberia to visit the grave of Saint Innocent of Irkutsk. It seemed to me that the Siberian forests and steppes would allow for quieter and more peaceful traveling and make it easier to pray and read. And so I set out, repeating the prayer continuously with my lips.

Finally, after a short time, I felt that the prayer began to move of its own accord from my lips into my heart. That is to say, it seemed as if my heart, while beating naturally, somehow began to repeat within itself the words of the prayer in rhythm with its natural beating: (1) Lord . . . (2) Jesus . . . (3) Christ . . . and so on. I stopped reciting the words of the prayer with my lips and began to listen attentively to the words of my heart, remembering what my starets said about how pleasant this would be. Then I began to experience a delicate soreness in my heart, and my thoughts were filled with such a love for Jesus Christ that it seemed to me that if I were to see Him, I would throw myself down, embrace His feet, and never let them go, kissing them tenderly and tearfully. And I would thank Him for His love and mercy in granting such consolation through His name to His unworthy and sinful creature!

Then a wholesome warmth began to fill my heart, and it seemed to spread throughout my chest. This warmth especially moved me to an attentive reading of the *Philokalia*, both to verify the feelings I had experienced and to further my studies of the interior prayer of the heart. I was afraid that without this verification I might fall into delusion or mistake natural activity for the action of grace and succumb to the pride, which the starets had spoken of, in having attained so quickly to this prayer.

So I took to walking mostly at night and spent my days sitting in the forest, under the trees, and reading the *Philokalia*. Ah, how much new knowledge, how much wisdom that I had never yet possessed, was revealed to me in this book! As I began to put it into practice, I tasted a sweetness I could not have even imagined until now. Although it is true that several passages I read were incomprehensible to my foolish mind, the effects of this prayer of the heart clarified what I'd failed to understand. At times my starets came to me in my dreams and explained so much to me. Above all else he inclined my ignorant soul toward humility. For more than two months of that summer I basked in this blissful state while I walked, keeping to the forests and the byroads. When I came to a village I would ask for dry bread to fill my knapsack with, and for a handful of salt. Then I would fill my bark jar with water, and on I would go for almost another seventy miles.

Perhaps it was due to the sins of my wretched soul, or for lack of something in my spiritual life, or the need for better guidance and more experience, but by the end of the summer I was assailed by temptations. On one such occasion I had come out onto a main road and was overtaken at dusk by two men, whose haircuts made me think they were soldiers. They began to demand money from me. When I replied that I didn't have a penny, they did not believe me and shouted insolently, "You're lying! Pilgrims always pick up a lot of money!" One of them said, "Don't waste your time arguing with him," and he clobbered me so hard over the head with a club that I fell down unconscious.

I don't know how long I lay unconscious, but when I came to I realized that I was lying near the forest, just off the road. I was disheveled and my knapsack was gone. All that was left were the severed ropes that had once held it on my back. Thank God they hadn't stolen my passport, which I carried inside my old hat, in case I needed to produce it quickly on demand. I stood up and burst into bitter tears, not so much from my aching head as over the fact that my books were gone—the Bible and the *Philokalia*, which were in the knapsack they had stolen.

So I grieved and wept day and night. Where was my Bible now, the one I had been reading from my early childhood and had always carried with me? Where was my *Philokalia*, which had given me such guidance and comfort? Woe is me, I had been deprived of the first and last treasures of my life—and I hadn't even had my fill of them yet! The robbers should have murdered me instead of leaving me to go on living without this spiritual nourishment. I would never replace it now!

For two days I barely dragged my feet, overwhelmed by my grief. By the third day I was so exhausted that I collapsed under a bush and fell asleep. I dreamed that I saw myself back at the monastery, in the cell of my starets, pouring out my grief to him. The starets comforted me and said, "Let this be a lesson to you in detachment from earthly material possessions; it will ease your journey toward heaven. This was permitted to happen to you so as to protect you from falling into spiritual gluttony. God wants from the Christian a complete denial of his own will, of his desires and of all attachment to them, so that he can totally submit himself to His Divine Will. He orders all things for the good and salvation of man: 'who desires all men to be saved . . .' [1 Tim. 2:4]. So take courage and believe that 'with the temptation God will also provide the way of escape' [1 Cor. 10:13]. And you will soon be comforted in far greater measure than you now grieve."

Upon hearing these words I awakened, feeling a new inner strength, and my soul was filled with light and peace. "God's will be done," I said, and making the sign of the cross over myself, I got up and went on my way. Once again the prayer came alive in my heart, just as it had done previously, and for three days I journeyed in peace.

Suddenly I caught up with a convoy of convicts, accompanied by a military escort. As I approached them I saw the two men who had robbed me. Since they were walking on the fringes of the convoy, I threw myself at their feet and earnestly begged them to tell me what they had done with my books. At first they ignored me, but then one of them said, "For a fee we'll tell you where your books are. Give us a ruble." I swore that I would pay them, even if I had to go begging for it, for Christ's sake. "Here—take my passport as a pledge, if you want," said I. They told me that my books were in the wagon in the rear, along with other stolen items that had been confiscated from them.

"How can I get them back?"

"Ask the captain in charge."

I hurried to the captain and told him my whole story. Among other questions, he asked me, "Can you really read the Bible?"

"Not only can I read," I replied, "but I can even write. You will see by the inscription in the Bible that it belongs to me. And here, my name and surname are in my passport too!"

Then the captain said, "These swindlers are military deserters. They were living in a mud hut and robbing everyone in sight. A clever coachman nabbed them yesterday as they tried to steal his three-horse team. I suppose I'll return your books to you, if they are here, but you'll have to accompany us to our next layover for the night. It's not far ahead, a little over two miles; we can't stop the wagon and the convoy just to get your books."

I walked gladly alongside the horse on which the captain rode and struck up a conversation with him. I noticed that he was an honest and kind man who was on in years. He asked me who I was, where I was headed, and where I hailed from. I answered all his questions honestly, and before long we had reached the hut where the convoy was to spend the night. He found my books, returned them to me, and said, "Where will you go now, in the dark? Spend the night here, in the foyer." So I stayed.

Now that the books were in my possession again, I was so happy that I knew not how to thank God. I clasped the books to my bosom and held them there until my arms went numb. Tears of joy streamed down my face and my heart beat tenderly with delight!

The captain had been watching me and said, "It's obvious that you love to read the Bible." I was so overjoyed that my tears spilled over and I could not answer him. "My brother, I also read the Bible faithfully each day," he said, and, unbuttoning his uniform jacket, he produced a small Bible that had been printed in Kiev and was bound in silver. "Sit down and I'll tell you what brought me to all this.

"How about some supper!" he shouted.

We sat down to eat and the captain began his story. "From the time I was a young man I have served in the army, not in a garrison unit. I knew my job and was a second lieutenant, well liked by my commanding officers. But I was young and so were my buddies, and unfortunately I started drinking heavily and eventually became an alcoholic. When I was sober, I was a model officer; but as soon as I hit the bottle again, I could not function for up to six weeks at a time. They put up with me for a long time until finally, in a drunken stupor, I insulted a commanding officer. I was demoted to the rank of soldier for three years, transferred to a garrison unit, and threatened with severe punishment if I did not straighten myself out and stop drinking. No matter how hard I tried to abstain in this miserable condition and no matter what cures I tried, I simply could not give up my addiction. Finally they decided to place me under military arrest, and when I heard this, I was at my wit's end.

"One day, as I sat in the barracks thinking, a monk came by unexpectedly, collecting alms for the church, and each of us gave whatever he could. As he approached me, he said, 'Why are you so sad?' We struck up a conversation, and I poured out all my woes to him. The monk expressed compassion for my plight and said, 'The very same thing happened to my brother. Here is what helped him: his spiritual father gave him a Bible and firmly instructed him that when he felt the urge to drink wine, he must pick up the Bible immediately and read a chapter from it. Each time the urge to drink returned, he was to read yet another chapter. My brother took his advice and, in a short time, his passion for alcohol disappeared. So for fifteen years now he has not had a drop of alcohol. Why don't you do the same? It'll work—you'll see. I have a Bible that I think I'll bring to you.'

"I listened to him and said, 'How can your Bible help me when neither my own efforts nor any medical cures succeeded in keeping me sober?' I said this because I had never read the Bible. The monk replied, 'Don't say that. I assure you that it will help.'

"The next day the monk indeed brought me his Bible. I opened it, looked inside, read some of it, and said, 'I won't accept it. I can't understand a single word of it. I'm not used to reading Church Slavonic.'* The monk continued to assure me that the very words of the Bible were imbued with the power of grace, for they were the words of God Himself. 'It does not matter if you don't understand it at first; just keep on reading diligently. A saint once said, "If you don't understand the words of God, at least the evil spirits understand what you read and they tremble before it." Your addiction to alcohol is certainly the work of the devil. Let me tell you something else: Saint John Chrysostom writes that even the very room where a Bible is kept frightens the spirits of darkness and makes it impossible for them to lay their evil snares.'

"I forget how much money I gave the monk, but I did accept his Bible. I then stored it away in a small trunk along with my other belongings and forgot about it. Sometime later I was overcome again by an irresistible urge to drink. I was dying for some wine, so I quickly opened my small trunk, to get some money and run over to the tavern. The first thing that my eyes fell upon was the Bible, and I clearly remembered all that the monk had told me. I opened it and began to read the first chapter of Matthew. I read the entire chapter without understanding a word of it. Then I remembered the monk's advice, 'If you don't understand it right away, keep on reading diligently.'

" 'All right,' I thought to myself, 'I'll read another chapter.' I read it and I began to understand. 'Why not try a third chapter?' I thought. But as soon as I started reading, the barracks bell sounded, announcing it was time to retire. It was obviously too late to go out, so I stayed put.

"When I arose in the morning, I was all ready to go for a drink when a thought struck me: 'I wonder what would happen if I read a chapter from the Bible?' I did just that and did not go out. Then again I felt the urge to drink wine. I again took to reading and felt much better. This encouraged me so much that each time I felt an urge to drink, I would read a chapter from the Bible. The more I did this, the easier it became to resist. Finally, when I had read through all four Gospels, the urge to drink had vanished to such a degree that I now felt an aversion to alcohol. It is now exactly twenty years that I have not touched a drop of any alcoholic beverage.

"Everyone was astonished by this transformation in me. Three years later my officer's rank was restored to me. In due time I was promoted again, until finally I attained the rank of commanding officer. I married a kind woman and we settled down. Now, thank God, we have a good life together; we give to the poor when we can, and we take in pilgrims. Why, my own son is already an officer—and a fine man he is!

"Listen: from the time I was healed of alcoholism, I made a vow to myself that for the rest of my life I would read the Bible, one Gospel every day, no matter how busy I was. So this is what I have been doing. On days when work runs me ragged, I come home, lie down, and make my wife or son read one of the Gospels to me, in its entirety, so as not to break my daily rule. In gratitude to God, and to His glory, I had this Bible bound in pure silver, and I always carry it with me, in my breast pocket."

I listened with delight to the captain's story and said, "I once knew someone who had the same experience. In our village there was a very gifted craftsman, who worked at the local factory. He was a kind man who did expensive work. Unfortunately, he also took to drinking frequently. A God-fearing man suggested to him that whenever he felt the urge to drink wine, he should repeat the Jesus prayer thirty-three times, in remembrance of the Holy Trinity and the thirty-three years of Jesus Christ's earthly life. The craftsman heeded this advice, started saying the prayer, and in no time he stopped drinking completely. And that was not all—three years later he entered a monastery!"

"Which is more exalted," asked the captain, "the Jesus prayer or the Bible?"

"It's all the same," I replied, "for the Divine Name of Jesus Christ contains within itself all the biblical truths. The holy Fathers say that the Jesus prayer is the abbreviated version of the entire Bible."

The two of us finally said our prayers, and the captain started reading from the Gospel of Saint Mark, chapter one. I listened, while in my heart I prayed the Jesus prayer. At two o'clock in the morning the captain finished reading the Gospel of Saint Mark, and we went to bed.

I rose early, as was my custom, and found that everyone was still asleep. At the first crack of dawn I threw myself into reading my precious *Philokalia*. What joy filled me as I opened that book! It was as if I'd been reunited, after a long separation, with my own father, or with a friend who had been resurrected from the dead. I covered the book with kisses and thanked God for restoring it to me, and immediately began to read Theophilus of Philadelphia, in the second part of the *Philokalia*. I was surprised to read that a man could simultaneously perform three different activities: "While sitting in the refectory," he writes, "give food to your body, give your attention to the reading of the day, and give your mind over to prayer." Yet when I remembered the joyful evening we had spent last night, my own living experience verified what I had just read. Thus, a mystery was revealed to me: namely, that the mind and the heart are separate entities.

When the captain arose, I went to thank him for his kindness and to take my leave of him. He offered me tea and gave me a ruble, and we parted. And I set off on my journey again, full of joy.

I had walked about three quarters of a mile when I remembered my promise to give those soldiers a ruble, which I now happened to have in my pocket. "Should I give it to them or not?" I wondered. One of my thoughts said, "They beat you up and robbed you. Besides, they're under arrest, so they couldn't even spend it." Another thought said, "Remember what the Bible says: 'If your enemy is hungry, feed him' [Rom. 12:20]. Even Jesus Christ Himself said, 'Love your enemies' [Matt. 5:44], and then: 'And if anyone would sue you and take your coat, let him have your cloak as well' " [Matt. 5:40]. This convinced me, and I decided to go back. As I approached the camp, all the criminals were being lined up outside for the next part of the journey. I hurried over to the two men, put the ruble piece in their hands, and said, "Repent and pray; Jesus Christ loves man; He will not abandon you!" Then I walked away and headed in the opposite direction.

The Way of a Pilgrim

I had walked a little over thirty-three miles along the main road when I thought of turning off onto a bypath so I could be alone to read. For a long time I walked through forests and only rarely ran across small villages. Often I spent an entire day sitting in the forest, carefully reading the *Philokalia* and learning so many wondrous things from it. My heart burned with a desire for union with God through interior prayer, which I strove to attain to under the guidance and verification of the *Philokalia*. Yet I also grieved that I had not yet found a permanent dwelling where I could spend all my time reading in peace.

During this time I also read my Bible and felt that I was beginning to understand it better than I had before, when so much was still unclear and puzzling to me. How right the Fathers are when they say the *Philokalia* is the key to unlocking the mysteries of Holy Scripture. With its guidance, I began to understand parts of the hidden meaning of the Word of God. The meanings of such statements as "the hidden inner man of the heart," "true prayer," "worshiping in the spirit," "the Kingdom of Heaven is within us," "the intercession of the Holy Spirit with unutterable groanings," "abide in me," "give me your heart," "to put on Christ," the "betrothal of the Spirit to our hearts," calling from one's heart: "Abba, Father!" and so on, were now being revealed to me. As I began to pray now with my heart, everything around me was so delightfully transformed: the trees, the grass, the birds, the ground, the air, the light—all seemed to proclaim that they exist for the sake of man and bear witness to the love of God for man. All creation prays to God and sings His praises. From this I understood what the *Philokalia* calls a "knowledge of the language of all creation," and I saw how it is possible for man to communicate with all of God's creatures.

I journeyed thus for a long time until, finally, I found myself in a place so uninhabited that for three days I did not see a single village. I had eaten all my dried bread, and I despaired at the thought that I would die of hunger. Yet as soon as I started praying, the despair would vanish. I gave myself over entirely to the will of God and was filled with joy and peace. When I had walked along part of the road that ran next to the forest, ahead of me I saw a mongrel dog come running out of the forest. It approached when I called to it and began to play affectionately with me. I was overjoyed and thought to myself, "Now there's God's mercy for you! Surely there must be a flock grazing in this forest, and of course this trained dog belongs to the shepherd; or perhaps there is a hunter nearby. Whatever the case, at least I'll be able to beg for some bread—I haven't eaten in twenty-four hours. Or else I can ask where the nearest village is."

The dog had been jumping around me, and when it

realized I had nothing to offer, it ran off into the forest down the same narrow path by which it had come out. I followed it, and about five hundred yards later I saw that the dog had run into a hole between some trees, from which it kept looking out and barking.

At that very moment a skinny, pale, middle-aged peasant emerged from behind a large tree. He asked me how I had come to be there and I, in turn, asked him what he was doing here. We struck up a friendly conversation, and the peasant invited me into his mud hut. He told me that he was a forester and was guarding this part of the woods, which had been sold for felling. He offered me bread and salt, and we began to talk. "I envy you," said I, "because you live in such comfortable solitude, so far removed from everyone, while I wander from place to place, mixing with all sorts of people."

"If you'd like to," he said, "maybe you can live here too. There's an old mud hut not far from here that belonged to the previous watchman. It's run down, of course, but it's livable in the summer. You have a passport, and we'll have enough bread to eat; they supply me with it weekly from the village. There's a stream here, which never dries up. For ten years now, brother, I myself have eaten only bread. I drink water and never anything else. There is one thing, however: in the fall, when the peasants finish working on the land, about two hundred of them will gather here to fell the trees in this forest. Then my job here will be over, and you won't be allowed to remain either."

When I heard all this, I was so overjoyed that I could have thrown myself at his feet. I knew not how to thank God for showing me such mercy. That which I'd desired and longed for was now being given to me so unexpectedly. There were still more than four months left until late fall. Here I could find the peace and solitude that I needed to immerse myself in reading the *Philokalia* and learning how to attain to the unceasing prayer of the heart. So I settled down joyfully in the hut he pointed out to me, for whatever time had been given me to live there. I talked some more with this simple brother who had offered me shelter, and he told me about his life and his thoughts on it.

"In my village," he said, "I had a good position; my trade was dyeing fustian and linen. I led a prosperous life, though not a sinless one. Often I cheated in business and took false oaths; I cursed, drank too much, and got into fights. There was an old deacon in our village who had an extremely old book about the Last Judgment. He would visit the Orthodox faithful and read to them from it, for which they gave him money. And he also visited me. Give him about ten kopecks and he could read into the night, till the cock crowed. So I'd sit and work, listening to him read about the torments that await us in hell, how the living would be transformed and the dead would be resurrected, how God would come down to judge us, how the angels would sound their trumpets, of the fire and brimstone, and how the worm would devour the sinners. One time, as I listened to all this, I got scared and thought to myself, 'There's no way I'll avoid that torment! Maybe it's time I started saving my soul—maybe I could even pray my sins away.' I thought about this for a long time and decided to give up my business. Since I had no family ties, I sold my hut and became a forester in exchange for being provided with bread, clothing, and candles for my prayers, by the village *mir*.*

"So I've lived here for more than ten years. I eat once a day, only bread with some water. I get up each day at the cock's crow and say my prayers and do my prostrations until dawn, burning seven candles in front of the icons. During the day, when I make my rounds of the forest, I wear iron chains weighing seventy-two pounds next to my skin. I don't curse anymore, or drink any wine or beer, or get into any fights, and I've never been with women or girls in my life.

"At first I preferred this kind of life, but lately I find myself constantly attacked by thoughts. God knows if sins can really be prayed away—and it is a hard life, you know. And then, is it really true what that book says—that dead men will be resurrected? Someone who died a hundred years ago or more—why, there's not even a speck of dust left of him. For that matter, who really knows if there will even be a hell, right? Why, no one has ever come back from the dead! It seems to me that once a man dies, he rots and vanishes without a trace. Maybe that book was written by the clergy, by some officials, just to scare us fools, to make us more humble. Life is full of hardships as it is, without any consolation—and there won't be anything in the next life. So what's the point? Isn't it better to take it easy, at least in this life, and to enjoy yourself? Such thoughts hound me," he continued, "and I wonder if I shouldn't just go back to my old job!"

Listening to him speak, I sympathized and thought to myself: they say that it is only the educated and the intelligent who are freethinkers and believe in nothing. But here is one of our own brethren—a simple peasant—and what doubts he is capable of entertaining! It appears that the powers of darkness are allowed access to everyone, and perhaps it is easier for them to attack the unsophisticated. A person must acquire wisdom and strengthen himself as much as possible with the Word of God against the spiritual enemy.

So as to help and strengthen this brother's faith as much as I could, I took the *Philokalia* out of my knapsack, opened it to chapter 109, the work of the venerable Hesychios, and read it to him. I then explained that abstaining from sin only because one fears pun-

ishment is a useless and fruitless task. "The soul cannot free itself from sins of thought other than by
guarding the mind and the purity of the heart, all of
which is achieved by interior prayer. Moreover," I
added, "the holy Fathers say that the efforts of those
who strive for salvation only from a fear of hell's torments, or even solely from a desire to enter the Kingdom of God, are mercenary. They say that to fear
suffering is the way of the servant, while to desire a
reward in the Kingdom is the way of the mercenary.
Yet God desires that we come to Him as sons, that we
be honest and delight in the redemptive union with
Him in our hearts and souls—but only out of love and
devotion to Him. No matter how you wear yourself out
with physical labors and struggles, if you do not keep
the remembrance of God in your mind and the Jesus
prayer in your heart, you will never find peace from
these thoughts and you will always be easily swayed
by sin, even by the smallest temptations. Why don't
you start saying the Jesus prayer, brother? It would be
possible and so easy to do with the solitude you live
in, and you will see its benefits in no time. No godless
thoughts will besiege you, and you will acquire faith
and love for Jesus Christ. Then you will know how it
is that the dead will be resurrected, and you will be
given to understand the Last Judgment as it really will
take place. Your heart will be so free of burdens and

so full of joy from this prayer that you will be amazed, and you'll no longer feel lonely or doubt the efforts you make toward your salvation."

Then I explained to him how to begin saying the Jesus prayer and how to repeat it continuously, as the Word of God instructs us and the holy Fathers teach us to do. It seemed to me that he was willing to do this and was much calmer now. I took leave of him then and shut myself up in the ancient mud hut that he had told me about.

My God! What joy, peace, and delight I knew the moment I set foot in that "cave," or better yet "tomb." It seemed to me to be the most magnificent palace, filled with every joy and consolation! I thanked God with tears of joy and thought, "Well, now, with all this peace and quiet I must seriously get back to my own task and ask the Lord to guide me." So I began by reading the *Philokalia* very carefully, starting with the first chapter and going all the way to the end. It did not take too long to read it through, and I realized what wisdom, holiness, and depth it contained. Yet it covered so many different subjects and contained so many different teachings of the holy Fathers that I was unable to understand everything or to piece together all that I wanted to learn, especially about interior prayer, so I could draw from it the knowledge of how to attain to the unceasing self-acting prayer of the heart. I longed for this, in keeping with God's commandment and as it was spoken through His apostle: "But earnestly desire the higher gifts" [1 Cor. 12:31] and again: "Do not quench the Spirit" [1 Thess. 5:19].

I thought about this for a long time. What could I do? I would start badgering the Lord with prayers; perhaps the Lord would somehow enlighten me. So I did nothing but pray continuously for the next twenty-four hours, not stopping for even a moment. My thoughts were calmed and I fell asleep. In my dream I saw myself sitting in the cell of my departed starets. He was explaining the *Philokalia* to me, saying, "This holy book is full of great wisdom. It is a mystical treasury of the meanings of the hidden judgments of God. It is not made accessible everywhere and to everyone, but it does offer instruction according to the measure of each reader's understanding. Thus, to the wise it offers wise guidance, while to the simpleminded it yields simple guidance. That is why you simpleminded ones should not read it section by section, in the order that the teachings of the different holy Fathers are printed in the book.

"First read the book of Nicephorus the Solitary (in part 2); then read the entire book of Saint Gregory of Sinai, excluding the short chapters; then read Simeon the New Theologian on the three kinds of prayer, and his Discourse on Faith; and afterward read the book of Callistus and Ignatius. The work of these Fathers contains the complete instruction and teaching on the interior prayer of the heart and can be understood by all.

"Then, if you should want an even clearer teaching on prayer, turn to section 4 for the summary on methods of prayer, by Callistus, the most holy Patriarch of Constantinople." In my dream I held the *Philokalia* in my hands and began to look for this passage, but I could not find it right away. The starets flipped through a few pages and said, "Here it is! I will mark the place for you." He picked up a piece of coal from the ground and made a mark with it in the margin, next to the passage he had found. I had listened carefully to everything the starets had said and tried to remember it in as much detail as possible. Since it was not yet dawn when I woke up, I lay in bed and went over every detail of my dream and everything the starets had told me. Finally I began to wonder, "God alone knows if this is really the soul of the late starets who is appearing to me in my dream, or if it is all in my mind, since I think so often about him and the *Philokalia*."

Still puzzled by all this, I got out of bed, for the light of day was dawning. And what do you think happened? I looked at the rock that served as a table in my mud hut and saw the *Philokalia* lying there, open to the very passage that the starets had pointed out to me, with the very markings he had made in charcoal! It was exactly as I had dreamed it—even the piece of coal lay next to the book! This astonished me, for I clearly remembered that the book had not been there the evening before; I had wrapped it up and placed it at the head of my bed. I was also quite sure that there had been no markings next to this specific passage. This incident finally convinced me of the reality of my dreams and that my starets of blessed memory had found favor in the eyes of God.

So I started reading the *Philokalia*, in the very order the starets had outlined for me. I read it through once and then a second time, and my soul burned with a desire and an eagerness to experience personally all that I had read about. The meaning of interior prayer was revealed clearly to my understanding: by what means one could attain to it, what were its fruits, how it delights the soul and the heart, and how to discern whether this sweet delight is from God, from natural causes, or the result of delusion.

So I began first to seek the place of the heart, according to the teaching of Simeon the New Theologian. I closed my eyes and gazed mentally into my heart; I tried to visualize it in the left part of my chest cavity and carefully listened to its beating. I began doing this exercise for half an hour, several times a day. At first I saw only total darkness, but soon a picture of my heart, along with the sound of its natural beating, formed in my mind. Then I began to repeat the Jesus prayer in my heart, in steady rhythm with my breathing, as taught by Saint Gregory of Sinai, Callistus, and Ignatius: namely, by concentrating my mind in the heart while visualizing it in my mind, I inhaled saying, "Lord Jesus Christ," and then exhaled saying, "Have mercy on me." At first I did this exercise for an hour or two. As I progressed, I increased the time, until finally I was able to repeat the exercise for almost the entire day. If weariness, laziness, or doubts assailed me, I immediately turned to reading the *Philokalia*, specifically those passages that deal with the work of the heart, and all desire and eagerness were restored.

After about three weeks I began to experience a soreness in my heart, followed by the most delightful kind of warmth, joy, and peace. This increasingly stirred me and kindled my desire to practice this prayer more diligently, so that I thought about nothing else and was filled with an immense joy. From then on, at times I would experience different sensations in my heart and in my mind. Sometimes my heart would bubble over with such sweet delight and was filled with such lightness, freedom, and consolation that I was totally transformed and enraptured. At other times I would be consumed with a burning love for Jesus Christ and for all of God's creation. Sometimes sweet tears of gratitude to the Lord, for His mercy to me a cursed sinner, would pour out of me of their own accord. And again, at times, my former foolish understanding was so illumined that suddenly I was able to ponder and comprehend so easily what previously I could not have even imagined. Sometimes the sweet warmth in my heart would overflow and spread through my entire being, so that I tenderly experienced the presence of God all about me. At other times I would experience the greatest inner joy from calling upon the name of Jesus Christ, and I realized the meaning of what He had said: "The Kingdom of God is within you" [Luke 17:21].

As I was experiencing these and other delightful consolations, I noticed that the effects of the prayer of the heart are manifested in three ways: in the spirit, in the feelings, and through revelations. In the spirit there is the sweetness of God's love, inner peace, the rapture of the mind, purity of thought, and the delightful remembrance of God. In the feelings there is a pleasant warming of the heart, a sweet delight that fills all the limbs, the heart bubbling over with joy, an inner lightness and vitality, the delight of being alive, and an inner detachment from illness and offenses. Revelations bring enlightenment of the intellect, an understanding of Holy Scripture, a knowledge of the language of all creatures, a detachment from all anxious cares, a taste of the sweet delights of the interior spiritual life, and a conviction in the close presence of God and in His love for us.

I spent about five months in the solitude of this

prayerful exercise, enjoying the experiences I described. I became so accustomed to the prayer of the heart that I practiced it continuously, until I finally felt that my mind and heart began to act and recite the prayer without any effort on my part. This continued not only when I was awake, but even as I slept, and nothing could interrupt it. It did not cease for even a moment, no matter what I happened to be occupied with. My soul was filled with gratitude to the Lord, while my heart languished in unceasing joy.

The time came for felling the trees in the forest, and the workers began to arrive. It was also time for me to leave my solitary abode. I thanked the forester, said a prayer, and knelt to kiss that plot of ground, which God had given to one as undeserving of His mercy as I am, to live on. I put my knapsack, containing the books, on my back and set out on my journey.

For a very long time I wandered through different places, until I arrived in Irkutsk. The self-acting prayer of the heart was my consolation and joy throughout the journey and in all my encounters. It never ceased to delight me, albeit in varying degrees. Wherever I happened to be, whatever I was doing, it never got in the way and was never diminished in any way at all. If I was working, the prayer flowed from my heart on its own and the work would go faster. If I was listening attentively to something or reading while the

The Way of a Pilgrim

prayer continued unceasingly, I would simultaneously be aware of both, as if I'd been divided in two or as if there were two souls in my one body. My God! What a mystery man is! "O, Lord, how wondrous are thy works! In wisdom hast thou made them all" [Ps. 104:24].

My travels were also filled with many wonderful experiences and incidents. Were I to recount them all, twenty-four hours would not suffice! But here is one example: it was dusk one winter evening as I walked alone in the forest. I was heading toward a village about a mile and a half ahead, where I planned to spend the night, when suddenly I was attacked by a wolf. In my hands I held the starets's old knotted wool chotki (I always carried them with me). I swung the knots to chase the wolf away—and what do you think happened? The chotki was whisked out of my hand and somehow became tangled right around the wolf's neck, and he took off. As he went crashing through a thorny bush, his back legs became tangled up in it, while the chotki caught on the branch of a dead tree. The wolf began to thrash about, but he could not free himself because the chotki had tightened around his throat. With faith I made the sign of the cross over myself and approached the wolf, intending to set him free, mainly because I feared that if he tore the chotki and ran off with it, then I would lose my precious chotki. Just as I came near and grabbed the chotki, it snapped, as the wolf broke loose and took off without a trace.

Thanking God, I prayed for my blessed starets and managed to get to the village safe and sound. I stopped at the inn, to ask for lodging for the night. As I entered the hut I saw two men sitting at a table in the corner and drinking tea. One was an old man, the other was fat and middle-aged, and neither appeared to be of the lower class. I asked the peasant tending their horses who they were. He said that the old man was a teacher in a public school and the other was a clerk of the county court; both were upper-crust people. "I'm taking them to a fair about thirteen miles from here," he said.

After sitting for a while, I asked a peasant woman for a needle and some thread and, moving closer to the candle, I began to mend my chotki. The clerk looked at me and said, "Looks like you did your prostrations with such zeal that your chotki broke!"

"It was not I who tore it," I replied; "it was a wolf."

The clerk chuckled and said, "My, my! Do wolves pray too?" I explained exactly what had happened in the forest and how precious the chotki was to me. The clerk laughed again and said, "Miracles always happen to you holy frauds! But where's the holiness in all this? You probably just threw something at the wolf and frightened him away. Dogs and wolves are afraid

The Way of a Pilgrim

of objects being hurled at them, and it doesn't take much to get caught in forest thickets. There's so much happening in this world—how can one believe that everything is a miracle?"

The teacher had been listening to the clerk and said to him, "Do not jump to such conclusions, sir! You are not familiar with the scholarly facts of the matter. I do see both the sensible and spiritual mystery of nature in this peasant's story."

"And how is that?" asked the clerk.

"Well, you see, although you lack a higher education, you must have studied a condensed version of the sacred history of the Old and New Testaments, the one that is published in catechism form for use in schools. Do you remember when the first created man, Adam, was in a state of innocent grace and all animals were obedient to him? They approached him with fear and he named each one. The starets to whom this chotki belonged was a holy man—and what is holiness? It is simply the return of sinful man, through efforts and struggles, to that innocent state of grace that the first man enjoyed. When the soul is sanctified, so is the body. Holy people always held chotki in their hands. This very contact of their hands and the holiness that emanated through them infused the knots with the power of the innocent state of the first man. That is the mystery of the spiritual nature of life! Down through the ages, and even to the present time, all animals naturally inherited the ability to sense this power. They experience it in their sense of smell, for the nose is the main organ of sensation in all beasts and animals. That is the mystery of the sensible nature of life!"

The clerk replied, "You educated people carry on about powers and wisdom! For us it's all much simpler: pour a shot of vodka, toss it down, and there's your power," and he got up and walked over to the cabinet.

"That is your business," said the teacher, "but leave scholarly matters to us."

I was pleased with the way the teacher had spoken, so I approached him and said: "If I may, Batyushka, I'd like to tell you more about my starets."

I told him of the dreams in which he had appeared to me, how he had instructed me and marked the passages in the *Philokalia* in charcoal. The teacher carefully listened to all this while the clerk, who was stretched out on a bench, grumbled: "It's like they say—you can lose your mind reading the Bible too much. How true that is! What ghost goes around at night, marking up books? You just knocked the book down on the floor in your sleep and it was smudged by some soot. There's your miracle! Oh, you scoundrels! I've seen enough of your kind!" Having mumbled this, the clerk turned to the wall and fell asleep.

I said to the teacher, "If you like, I'll show you that

very book and you'll see that it has precise markings in it and not just sooty smudges." I took the *Philokalia* out of my knapsack and showed it to him, saying, "I marvel at such wisdom; how could a bodiless soul pick up a piece of charcoal and write with it?"

The teacher looked at the markings and replied, "That belongs also to the realm of spiritual mysteries. Let me explain this: you see, when spirits appear in bodily form to someone on earth, they fashion a material body for themselves from the air and elements around them. Once their task is done they return the elements to the material world, from which they were borrowed to create the bodies. Just as the air is resilient, has elasticity, and can be compressed, so the soul clothed in it can pick up material objects and perform actions such as writing. By the way, what is that book you have there? Let me see it!"

He opened the book at random to the writing of Saint Simeon the New Theologian. "Ah, this must be a theological work; I've never seen it before."

"Batyushka, this book consists almost solely of teachings on the interior prayer of the heart in the name of Jesus Christ," I replied. "It is explained in complete detail here by twenty-five holy Fathers."

"I do know about interior prayer," said the teacher. I bowed to the ground before him and asked him to tell me something about interior prayer.

"This is what the New Testament says: man and all

creation are subject to 'vanity, not of [their] own will,' and 'groan inwardly, struggling and desiring to enter into the liberty of the sons of God' [Rom. 8:20ff]. Interior prayer is this mystical inward groaning of creation and the innate aspiration of souls toward God. It is not something that needs to be learned, for it is innate in everyone and everything!"

"How can one attain to it, discover it, and experience it in the heart?" I asked. "How can one recognize and accept it with one's will, and acquire it so that it becomes active, to delight, to enlighten, and to save a person?"

"I do not remember if this is written about in any theological treatises," replied the teacher.

"But here—it is all written here," I said.

The teacher picked up a pencil, jotted down the title of the *Philokalia,* and said, "I simply must order this book from Tobolsk, so I can study it." Then we took leave of each other.

As I started again on my journey, I thanked God for that conversation with the teacher, but I prayed for the clerk, that the Lord would somehow arrange that he read the *Philokalia* at least once and grant him wisdom for his salvation.

Another time, it was in the spring that I came to a village where I found lodging for the night at a priest's house. He was a kind man and lived alone, so I spent three days with him. After observing me during this time, he said, "Stay here with me. I need a conscientious man here, and I'll pay you a wage. You see that we are building a new stone church, near the old wooden chapel. I have not been able to find a reliable man to keep an eye on the workers and to sit in the chapel, accepting donations for the new building. You could handle this, and it would suit your way of life. You could sit alone in the chapel and pray to God. There is also a separate booth for the watchman to sit in. Please stay, at least until the new church is built." I tried to get out of doing this, but the priest was so insistent that finally I had to agree.

Through the summer I lived in that chapel, until the fall came. At first it was peaceful and very conducive to reciting my prayer, even though many people visited the chapel, especially on feast days. Some came to pray, some to dawdle, while others came to steal from the collection plate. I regularly read the Bible and the *Philokalia,* and when visitors saw this, some would strike up a conversation with me. Others would merely ask me to read to them.

After a while I noticed that a young peasant girl came frequently to the chapel and spent a long time praying to God. I listened to her muttering and discovered that some of the prayers she was repeating were very odd-sounding, while others seemed to be completely distorted. "Who taught you all this?" I asked. She replied that her mother, who was a churchgoing woman, had taught her. Her father was a schismatic who belonged to a sect that rejected the priesthood. I sympathized with all this and then advised her to pray according to the proper tradition of the holy church: namely, the Lord's Prayer and "Rejoice O Virgin Theotokos."* Finally, I said, "Why don't you make a habit of saying the Jesus prayer? It reaches out to God more directly than any other prayer, and through it you will attain salvation for your soul."

The young girl took my advice seriously and very simply began doing what I had taught her. And do you know what happened? After a short time she informed me that she had become so accustomed to the Jesus prayer that she felt drawn to reciting it continuously, if such a thing were possible, and that while she prayed she was filled with gladness, whereas when she stopped, she was filled with joy and a desire to pray again. I was overjoyed by this and advised her to continue praying in the name of Jesus Christ.

The end of the summer was drawing near. Many of the visitors to the chapel were now coming to see me. They came not only to hear me read to them and for advice, but they also brought all their problems to me, even seeking help in locating misplaced or lost items. Obviously, some of them took me for some sort of fortuneteller. Finally, the same young girl came back, filled with grief and seeking advice. What should she do? Her father had decided to marry her off, against her will, to one of the schismatics in his sect, and the wedding was to be performed by one of the peasants. "How could that be a legal marriage?" she cried. "It will be nothing but debauchery! I want to run away—it doesn't matter where I go!"

"Where would you run?" I asked. "They'll only find you again. Nowadays, there is nowhere you could hide yourself well enough. No matter where you go, they will find you. Why don't you pray to God more earnestly about this and rely on His judgment about changing your father's mind and saving your soul from sin and heresy? That would be far more sensible than running away."

As time went on, life became unbearably noisy for me and full of distracting temptations. Finally the summer was over and I decided to leave the chapel to continue on my own journey. I went to the priest and said, "Batyushka, you know what I am seeking. I need quiet surroundings to pray, and there are too many harmful distractions here. I have fulfilled by obedience to you and stayed through the summer. Release me now and give me your blessing for my solitary journey."

The priest did not want to let me go, and he tried to convince me to stay. "What's stopping you from praying right here? There's nothing for you to do here except to sit in the chapel. Your daily bread is provided for you. Say your prayers there day and night, if you like, and live with God, brother! You are very gifted, and your presence here is good for us. You don't gossip idly with visitors, and you are doing something profitable for God's church by faithfully taking in the collections. This is more pleasing to God than your prayers in solitude. What do you need solitude for? It's merrier to pray in community with others. God did not create man so that he could get to know only himself, but so that people would help each other, lead each other to salvation according to each one's abilities. Take a look at the saints and the ecumenical Fathers! They were concerned and cared for the Church day and night and traveled all over to preach. They did not go off in solitude and hide from people."

"God gives to each man his own gift, Batyushka. There have been many preachers, but there have also been many hermits. Each found his own unique calling and followed it, believing that through this God Himself was guiding him on the path to salvation. How then would you explain the fact that so many saints gave up their ecclesiastical offices, administrative positions, and priestly duties and fled into the solitude of the desert, to avoid the confusion and distractions of living among people? Saint Isaac the Syrian fled, leaving behind his episcopal diocese. The venerable Athanasius of Athos fled from his large monastery. They did this precisely because those places were too

The Way of a Pilgrim

distracting, too full of temptations for them, and because they genuinely believed the words of Jesus Christ: 'For what will it profit a man, if he gains the whole world and forfeits his life?' " [Matt. 16:26].

"But they were saints!" said the priest.

"If the saints needed to protect themselves from the dangers of mingling with people," I replied, "then what must a poor sinner resort to!"

In the end I finally parted with this kind priest, and he lovingly saw me on my way.

After walking almost seven miles I stopped for the night in a village. At the inn I found a peasant who was extremely ill, and I advised his friends that he should receive his last communion. They agreed, and by morning they had sent for the priest from the village parish. I remained so that I could venerate the holy gifts and pray while this great sacrament was administered. In the meanwhile I went out into the street and sat down on a mound of earth to wait for the priest. Suddenly I saw a young girl running toward me from the backyard—the one who had spent so much time praying at the chapel.

"How did you end up here?" I asked.

"The date was set for my betrothal to that schismatic," she replied, "so I left." Then she bowed to the ground before me and said, "Be merciful—let me go with you and take me to some women's monastery! I don't want to be married. I'll live in a monastery and pray the Jesus prayer. They'll take me in on your word."

"Mercy!" I said. "And just where am I going to take you? I don't know a single women's monastery in this part of the country. Besides, how could I take you with me when you don't even have a passport? For one thing, no one will take you in anywhere, and for another, you won't be able to hide anywhere nowadays. You would be caught at once and sent back home, and they may even punish you for vagrancy. Why don't you just go home and pray to God, and if you don't want to get married, then make up some illness as an excuse. That's called pretending for the sake of salvation. The holy Mother Clementa did this, and so did the blessed Marina when she took refuge in a men's monastery. And there were also many others."

While we were sitting and talking, we saw four peasants come tearing down the road toward us in a wagon. They grabbed the girl, put her in their wagon, and sent her off with one of the peasants. The other three tied my hands together and forcibly led me back to the village where I had just spent the summer. I tried to explain the situation to them, but they kept shouting, "We'll teach you to seduce our girls, little holy man!" We arrived toward evening, and they took me to the village courthouse, chained my legs, and locked me up in a jail cell to await trial in the morning. The priest found out that I was in jail and came to visit me. He brought me some dinner, and in an attempt to comfort me he said that, as my spiritual father, he would testify on my behalf and tell them that I was not the kind of man to do what they were accusing me of. He stayed with me for a while and then departed.

Later that evening, the magistrate happened to be riding through the village on his way somewhere. He stopped to see the village deputy and was informed of what had happened. He gathered everyone together and ordered me brought to the courthouse. We went and stood there, waiting for him. The magistrate arrived in high spirits; he sat down at the table, still wearing his hat, and shouted, "Hey, Epiphan! The girl—your daughter—she didn't steal anything from your house, did she?"

"No, Batyushka, nothing!"

"Has she been caught in any funny business with that fool over there?"

"No, Batyushka!"

"Fine! Then this is my decision on how we're going to settle this: you handle your own daughter. As for this young know-it-all, we'll teach him a lesson tomorrow and chase him out of the village. He'll be told in no uncertain terms never to come back here again. That's all!"

Having passed this judgment, the magistrate stood

up and went home to sleep, while I was returned to the jail. Two village policemen came in the morning, gave me a thrashing, and let me go. I left, thanking God that He had deemed me worthy to suffer for His name. This comforted me greatly and further kindled the unceasing prayer of my heart.

I was not offended by anything that had happened to me. It was as if it had happened to someone else and I had been merely an observer. Even the beating I received was within my power to endure. The prayer that delighted my heart made me unaware of everything else.

After walking almost three miles, I met the young girl's mother, who was on her way home with purchases from the market. She saw me and said, "Our bridegroom has backed off from the marriage. You see, he was angry with Akulka for running away from him." Then she gave me some bread and a patty, and I went on my way.

The weather was dry, and I had no desire to spend the night in another village. So that evening, when I saw two fenced-in haystacks in the forest, I settled down under them for the night. When I fell asleep, I dreamed that I was walking along the road and reading chapters from the work of Saint Anthony the Great in the *Philokalia*. Suddenly the starets caught up with me and said, "You're reading the wrong passage. This is what you should read," and he pointed to the thirty-fifth chapter of Saint John of Karpathos, where I read the following: "Sometimes the teacher submits to ignominy and suffers temptations for the sake of those who will benefit spiritually from this." The starets also pointed out the forty-first chapter, by the same Saint John, which said: "Those who pray most earnestly are the ones who are assailed by the most terrible and fierce temptations."

Then the starets said, "Be strong in spirit and do not despair! Remember what the apostle said: '. . . He who is in you is greater than he who is in the world' [1 John 4:4]. Now you have experienced for yourself that a man is tempted only as much as he can endure it; 'but with the temptation God will also provide the way of escape' [1 Cor. 10:13]. Hoping in God's help is what strengthened holy men of prayer and led them on to zeal and fervor. Such men not only gave their lives over to unceasing prayer, but out of their love they also revealed and taught it to others, whenever the opportunity presented itself. Saint Gregory of Thessalonika says the following about this: 'It is not only we who should heed God's command to pray unceasingly in the name of Christ. We must also reveal and teach this prayer to others, to everyone, in fact: monastics, lay people, the wise, the simple, husbands, wives, and children. We must awaken in them a desire to pray unceasingly.' The venerable Callistus Telicudis says something very similar: 'Neither mental prayer to the

Lord [i.e., interior prayer] nor contemplative illumination nor any means of elevating one's soul should be hoarded in one's own mind. They must be recorded, written down, and made available to others for the sake of love and the common good of all.' The Scriptures themselves speak of this: 'Brother helped by brother is like a strong fortress' [Prov. 18:19]. However, in this case one should flee vanity in every possible way and guard oneself, so that the seed of God's Word is not sown into the wind."

When I awakened, my heart was filled with great joy and my soul was strengthened, and I went on my way.

After this, a long time passed before another incident occurred. Perhaps I will tell you about it. It was on March 24 when I experienced an irresistible desire to receive Holy Communion on the following day, which was the Feast of the Annunciation of the Most Pure Theotokos. I asked for the whereabouts of the local church and was told that it was twenty miles away. So for the rest of that day and night I walked, in order to get to matins on time. The weather could not have been worse. First it snowed, then it rained; the wind was strong and it was very cold. Along the way I had to cross a small creek, and when I reached the middle of it, the ice broke under my feet and I fell into the water up to my waist. When I arrived for matins I was soaked, but I stood through matins and then the

Divine Liturgy, at which God had granted me to receive Communion.

In order to spend that day peacefully, without disturbing the spiritual joy that filled me, I asked the church watchman if I could spend the night in his room. That entire day my heart was filled with indescribable joy and delight. I lay on the plank bed in this unheated room as if I were resting in the bosom of Abraham, while the prayer flowed intensely. A love for Jesus Christ and the Mother of God washed over my heart in waves of delight and steeped my soul in a soothing rapture. Toward evening I suddenly felt a strong pain in my legs and remembered that they were still wet. I ignored this and listened more attentively to the prayer in my heart, and soon I no longer noticed the pain. The next morning I tried to get out of bed and realized that I could not move my legs. They were completely paralyzed, as weak as if they were limp pieces of string. The watchman was barely able to drag me off the bed. For two days I sat, unable to walk, and on the third day the watchman began to chase me out from his room, saying, "If you die here, who's going to bury you?" Somehow I barely managed to crawl out of there, dragging myself on the ground with my hands, and collapsed on the church steps, where I lay for about two days. People walked right past me, completely ignoring me and my pleas for help.

Finally some peasant came up to me, sat down, and

struck up a conversation. "What will you pay me if I cure you?" he asked. "The exact same thing once happened to me, so I know the cure."

"I have nothing to give you," I said.

"What have you got there in your knapsack?"

"Only some dried bread and books."

"Well, how about working for me, for at least one summer, if I cure you?"

"I can't do any work. You see that I have the use of only one arm, and the other one is almost completely withered."

"So what can you do?"

"Nothing, really—but I do read and write."

"Aha, you can write! Well, then, teach my son. He reads a little, and I want him to learn to write. But tutors are expensive—they want twenty rubles to teach him." I agreed to this, and with the watchman's help the peasant dragged me off and put me in an old abandoned bathhouse in his backyard.

Then he set about curing me. He scoured the fields, yards, and garbage dumps and gathered almost a bushel of rotting bones: bird and cattle bones, among others. He washed them, ground them down with a rock, and placed them in a large earthen pot. He covered this with a lid with a small opening in it and lowered it upside down into an empty jar sunk in the ground. He smeared the lid of the earthen pot with a thick layer of clay. Then he made a pile of wood around it and lit a fire, which he kept burning for more than twenty-four hours. As he added wood to the fire, he said, "Now we'll get some tar from these bones."

The next day he dug the jar out of the ground. It contained a little over a pint of viscous liquid that had dripped into it through the hole in the lid of the earthen pot. It was a reddish, oily liquid that smelled abominably, like raw meat. The bones, which had initially been black with putrefaction, were now clean and white—as transparent as mother-of-pearl, or actual pearls. I rubbed this liquid into my legs five times a day. And what do you think? On the second day I was able to wiggle my toes. On the third day I could bend and unbend my knees. On the fifth day I walked around the yard with the help of a cane. In a word, by the end of a week my legs had recovered their former strength! I thanked God for all this and thought to myself: what wisdom has gone into God's creation! That those dry, rotting, almost completely decomposed bones could contain such vital power, color, and odor and have such an effect on living organisms, as if bringing life to deadened limbs! This is indeed a pledge of the coming resurrection. If only that forester, with whom I spent the summer and who doubted the final resurrection of all life, could see this now!

Once I was cured, I began teaching the little boy. Instead of using a grammar book, I wrote out the Jesus prayer, showed him how to form the letters, and had him copy it. Teaching the boy was very restful for me, because during the day he was apprenticed to a local estate steward and could study with me only while the steward slept, from daybreak until the late-morning Liturgy. He was a bright boy and was soon able to write a few things fairly well. When the steward found out that the boy could write, he asked him, "Who is teaching you?" The boy replied, "A pilgrim with a disabled arm who is staying with us in the abandoned bathhouse."

The curious steward, who was Polish, came to see me and found me reading the *Philokalia*. He started talking with me and asked, "What are you reading?" I showed him the book. "Ah," he said, "that's the *Philokalia*! I saw this book at our *ksenda's** when I lived in Vilna. I once heard that it contains some very strange magic and methods for praying that were written down by Greek monks and that are similar to what those fanatics in India and Bukhara do. They sit and breathe up a storm so they can experience some stirring in their hearts, and in their stupidity, they mistake these natural feelings for prayer, thinking that they are given to them by God Himself. We should pray simply because this is our obligation before God. Get up in the morning, say the Our Father as Christ taught us, and you're set for the whole day—but not this endless repetition, beating the same thing to death, over and over again! Why, you could go out of your mind—and hurt your heart in the process!"

"Do not think that way about this holy book, Bat-yushka," I replied. "It was not written by ordinary Greek monks, but by the greatest and holiest men of long ago, who are revered by your Church as well: Saint Anthony the Great, Saint Macarius the Great, Mark the Anchorite, Saint John Chrysostom, and others. It was from them that the monks of India and Bukhara adopted the method for interior prayer of the heart, but my starets told me that they distorted and ruined it. But in the *Philokalia*, all the teachings on the prayer of the heart are rooted in the Word of God, the Holy Bible, where the same Jesus Christ Who taught us the Our Father, also commanded us to pray unceasingly, saying, 'Love the Lord your God with all your heart and all your mind' [Matt. 22:37]; 'Take heed, watch . . . and pray' [Mk. 13:33]; 'Abide in me and I in you.' [Jn. 15:4] And the holy Fathers cite the witness King David bears in the Psalter: 'O taste and see that the Lord is good!' (Ps. 34:8). They explain this by saying that the Christian must do everything possible to acquire and experience the delights of prayer, continually seeking the consolation it brings—and not just say the Our Father once a day. Here, let me read to you how these saints condemn those who do not strive to learn and practice the delightful prayer of the heart. They write that such people make the following mistakes: they contradict the divinely inspired Scriptures; they do not set their sights upon a higher and more perfect spiritual state for their souls and, instead, are satisfied only with external good works; they do not hunger and thirst for the truth, thus depriving themselves of bliss and joy in the Lord; because they judge themselves on the basis of their external works, they frequently fall into delusion or pride and alienate themselves."

"What you are reading is quite lofty," said the steward, "but it hardly applies to us ordinary people who live in the world!"

"Here, let me read you something simpler, about how even good people, living in the world, managed to learn unceasing prayer." I found a passage from Saint Simeon the New Theologian in the *Philokalia*, about George the Younger, and read it to him.

The steward was impressed by this and said, "Let me borrow this book and I'll look through it when I have some free time."

"I suppose I could give it to you for twenty-four hours, but no longer, because I read it daily and cannot manage without it."

"Well, at least copy out what you just read. I'll pay you for it."

"I don't need your money. I'll copy it for the sake

of love, and I only hope that God will grant you the desire to practice this prayer."

With great pleasure I immediately copied the passage I had read, and he took it home and read it to his wife. They were both impressed by it and began inviting me over. I would go, bringing the *Philokalia* with me, and read to them while they drank tea and listened. One time they asked me to stay for dinner. The steward's wife, a kind elderly woman, sat with us as we ate fried fish. Suddenly she choked on a fish bone and, after trying everything possible, we could not get it out. She had a great deal of pain in her throat, and after about two hours took to her bed. We sent for the doctor, who lived thirty miles away, but since it was already evening, unfortunately I had to go home.

I slept lightly that night and dreamed that I heard my starets's voice. I could not see him, but I heard him say, "Your landlord cured you—and you can't even help the steward's wife? God commanded us to have compassion for our neighbor's suffering."

"I'd be more than glad to help—but how? I don't know what to do!"

"Here is what you do: the old lady has a lifelong aversion to lamp oil. Not only is she unable to swallow it, but she cannot abide even the smell of it without getting nauseated. So you must get her to swallow a spoonful of the lamp oil, and this will induce vomiting and dislodge the bone. The oil will also coat the wound that the bone made in her throat, and it will heal."

"But how will I get her to take lamp oil if she has such an aversion to it? She won't swallow it!"

"You tell the steward to hold her head while you quickly pour it down her throat. Use force if you have to."

When I woke up I went at once to the steward's home and told him all this in detail. "What good will your oil do now?" he said. "Her throat is already hoarse, she's hallucinating, and her neck is all swollen! But then again, maybe we should give it a try. Oil is a harmless medicine, even though it won't do any good either."

He poured some lamp oil into a shot glass, and somehow we managed to get her to swallow it. The vomiting started immediately, and soon the fish bone came out, along with some blood. She felt better and fell into a deep sleep.

I came back in the morning to check on her and saw that she was calmly drinking tea. Both she and her husband were astonished by this cure, but especially by the fact that the wife's aversion to lamp oil had been revealed to me in a dream, for they alone knew about this. At that point the doctor arrived and the steward's wife told him what had happened to her, while I described how the peasant had cured me. After listening to us, the doctor said, "Neither case is all that unusual. The same natural powers were active in both instances. However, let me write it down so I don't forget it." He produced a pencil and made some notes in his notebook.

After this incident, word spread quickly around the neighborhood that I was a visionary, a healer, and a witch doctor. People started coming to me from all over with their affairs and problems. They brought me gifts, began to treat me with great respect, and looked after all my comforts. I put up with this for a week, but then I became afraid of falling into vainglory and being harmed by all these distractions. So I left during the night without saying a word to anyone.

Thus I embarked once again on my solitary journey. I experienced such a lightness within me, as if an immense burden had been removed from my shoulders. The prayer increasingly comforted me, so that often my heart would bubble over with boundless love for Jesus Christ. Gentle streams of consolation would flow from this delight through all the joints in my body. The remembrance of Jesus Christ was so engraved in my mind that when I meditated on biblical events it was as if I could see them right before my very eyes. I was filled with a warm tenderness and shed tears of joy. Such joy filled my heart that I have no words to describe it!

At times I would go for three whole days without encountering any human habitation, which, to my immense delight, made me feel as if I were the only man alive on earth—one wretched sinner in the presence of the merciful and man-loving God. This solitude consoled me and enabled me to experience the delights of the prayer with far greater sensitivity than I do when I am surrounded by people.

Finally I arrived in Irkutsk. There I venerated the relics of Saint Innocent and began to think to myself, "So, where do I go from here?" I had no desire to stay there for any length of time, for the city was heavily populated. I walked down the street, lost in my thoughts, when I met one of the local merchants. He stopped me and asked, "Are you a pilgrim? Why don't you come over to my house?" I went, and soon we arrived at his lavish house. He asked me about myself and I told him about my travels. When I had finished, he said, "It is to old Jerusalem that you should make a pilgrimage. The shrines and relics there cannot compare to anything else in the world!"

"I would gladly go," I replied, "but there is no way to get there by land. I could get as far as the sea, but I cannot pay for a sea voyage. I would need some money for that."

"If you like," said the merchant, "I could make it possible for you to go. Just last year I sent one of our old-timers there."

I fell at his feet and he said, "Listen here, I'll give you a letter of introduction to my son. He lives in

Odessa and does business with Constantinople, so his ships sail there. He will gladly arrange passage for you on one of his vessels. Then in Constantinople he will instruct his agents to book passage for you on another ship that sails to Jerusalem and to pay for it. It's not all that expensive."

When I heard this I was overcome with joy. I showered my benefactor with gratitude for his kindness. Then I thanked God for the fatherly love and care that He had bestowed on such a wretched sinner as I, who was no good to himself or to others, and who ate the bread of others in idleness.

I enjoyed the hospitality of the generous merchant for three days, and he provided me with the promised letter of introduction to his son. So there I was, on my way to Odessa, in hope of reaching the holy city of Jerusalem. Yet I did not even know for sure if the Lord would grant me to venerate his life-giving tomb.

THIRD
NARRATIVE

J UST BEFORE LEAVING IRKUTSK I visited my spiritual father, with whom I had spoken frequently, and said to him, "Well, here I am, off to Jerusalem. I just came to say good-bye and to thank you for the Christian love you have shown to me, an unworthy pilgrim."

"May God bless your journey," he replied. "But you know, you have not told me all that much about yourself—who you are, where you are from. You told me so much about your travels, I would be curious to know where you are from and about your life before you became a pilgrim."

"Of course," I said, "I'll be glad to tell you about that too. My story is not all that long. I was born in a village in the Orlovsk province. After my parents died, there were just the two of us left—I and my older brother. He was ten years old and I was two, going on three. Our grandfather took us in to raise us. He was a prosperous and honest old man who kept an inn on the main thoroughfare, and thanks to his kindness many a traveler stayed at the inn. So we went to live with him.

My brother was very high-spirited and often took off on his own, running around the village, while I spent more time with Grandfather. On feast days we attended church with him, and he often read from the Bible at home—in fact, from this very same one that I now carry with me. When my brother got older, something went wrong in his life, and he took to drinking heavily. I was seven years old at the time. I remember that once, when we were lying down together on the stove, he pushed me off and I hurt my left arm when I fell. After that I lost the use of this arm, and now it has all withered up.

"Grandfather realized that I would not be able to work on the land, so he began to teach me to read and write. Since we had no grammar books, he somehow managed to use this very Bible instead. He started from the very beginning and had me writing words so I could learn the letters of the alphabet. I do not know how I did it, but by repeating everything he said, I eventually learned how to read. Finally, when Grandfather's vision grew weak, he frequently made me read to him from the Bible, correcting me as I went along.

"There was a county clerk who often stayed at the inn, and he had such a beautiful handwriting. I enjoyed watching him write and tried to copy his writing. He began to teach me, giving me paper and ink and sharpening my quills. That was how I learned to write. Grandfather was very pleased by this and would say to me, 'Now that God has revealed reading and writing to you, it will make a man out of you. You must thank the Lord for this and pray more often.' So we would attend all the church services, but we also prayed a great deal at home. I would chant 'Have mercy on me, O God,' while Grandfather and Grandmother did their prostrations or simply knelt.

"Finally, when I turned seventeen, Grandmother died. Grandfather would say to me, 'We don't have a mistress of the house any longer—how are we going to manage without a woman? Your older brother has made a mess of his life, so I want you to get married.' I protested because of my disabled arm, but Grandfather insisted. They found a mature, kind twenty-year-old girl for me and we were married.

"One year later, Grandfather became ill and was on his deathbed when he called for me. As he spoke words of parting, he said, 'I am leaving you this house and everything I own. Live by your conscience, do not cheat anyone, but above all else pray to God, for everything comes from Him. Do not place your hope in anything or anyone, but only in God. Go to church, read the Bible, and remember me and the old lady in your prayers. I am giving you a thousand rubles. Be careful with the money and do not spend it foolishly, but neither be stingy with it. Give to God's Church and to His poor.'

"So he died and I buried him. My brother grew very

The Way of a Pilgrim

jealous because I alone had inherited the inn and the rest of the estate. He became enraged with me and was so enmeshed in evil that he actually plotted to kill me. Finally, this is what he did one night, while we were sleeping. There were no guests at the inn, and he broke into the closet where I kept the money, stole it from the chest, and set fire to the closet. By the time we awakened, the fire had spread through the whole hut and inn. We barely managed to jump out the window, wearing nothing but our nightclothes.

"Since we kept the Bible under our pillows, we were able to take it with us. As we stood and watched our house burning, we said to each other, 'Thank God, at least we rescued the Bible! At least we have something to console us in our distress.' Thus our entire estate burned down and my brother disappeared without a trace. Much later we found out that he had begun to drink heavily and was heard to boast about how he had stolen the money and had set fire to the inn.

"We were left completely destitute, without any clothing or even a pair of *lapti** to wear. Somehow we managed to borrow some money to build a small cabin, and we started living in it as landless peasants. My wife did beautiful handiwork—weaving, spinning, sewing. She took in work, laboring day and night to support me. With my withered arm I could not even make shoes, so I would sit while she wove or spun and read to her from the Bible. She would listen and sometimes burst into tears. 'Why are you crying?' I'd ask. 'Thank God that at least we are alive.' And she would reply, 'The Bible contains such beautiful words that it touches me so deeply.'

"Remembering Grandfather's admonitions, we fasted frequently, chanted the akathist to the Theotokos every morning, and did one thousand prostrations before going to bed at night, so as not to fall into temptation. Thus we lived peacefully for two years. It is interesting that although we had never heard of the prayer of the heart, did not understand it, and simply prayed with our lips, doing mindless prostrations like blockheads performing somersaults, we still had the desire to pray. Not only was it easy for us to recite long prayers without really understanding them, but we did so with great delight. It seems that teacher was right when he told me that one could pray secretly within himself, without being consciously aware of the prayer or of how it acts on its own in the soul and awakens the desire to pray, according to each person's knowledge and ability.

"After living this way for two years, my wife suddenly became ill with a very high fever. She received her last Communion and died on the ninth day of her illness. I was left completely alone, without any means of supporting myself. So I started wandering about and begging, of which I was quite ashamed. In addition, I was overwhelmed with such grief over losing my wife that I didn't know what to do with myself. When I walked into my cabin and saw her clothing or a kerchief she wore, I would let out such a howl and even faint. Finally it became impossible for me to bear my grief living at home. So I sold my hut for twenty rubles and gave to the poor whatever was left of my wife's and my clothing. Because of my arm, I was given a permanent disability passport, and I took my Bible and set off without any specific destination in mind.

" 'Where will I go now?' I thought. 'I'll go to Kiev first, to venerate the relics of God's worthy saints and ask for their help and intercession.' This decision instantly made me feel much better, and my journey to Kiev turned out to be a joyous one. This was thirteen years ago, and ever since then I have been wandering through different places. I have visited many churches and monasteries, but nowadays I keep mainly to the steppes and fields. I am not sure if the Lord has ordained it for me to reach the holy city of Jerusalem. If it is God's will, perhaps it is time for my sinful bones to be buried there."

"How old are you now?"

"I'm thirty-three."

"The age of Jesus Christ at His death!"

FOURTH
NARRATIVE

But for me it is good to be near God; I have made the
Lord God my refuge. . . .

—Ps. 73:28

WHEN I CAME TO my spiritual father I said,
"How true it is what that Russian proverb
says: 'Man proposes, but God disposes.' I
had planned to set out today and start on my journey
to the city of Jerusalem. However, something quite different happened. A totally unforeseen incident has
kept me here for three more days. I could not resist
coming to see you, to tell you about this, for I needed
your advice on how to handle it. I will tell you about
this unexpected incident.

"After I had taken my leave of everyone, with God's
help I set out on my journey. Just as I was about to
pass through the gates of the city, I saw a familiar man
standing at the doorway of the last house. He was once
a pilgrim, just as I am, and I had not seen him for
three years. We greeted each other, and he asked me
where I was headed.

"I replied, 'I'd like to get to the old Jerusalem, God
willing.'

" 'Thank God!' he exclaimed. 'I know a good traveling companion for you.'

" 'God be with you and with him,' I said, 'but surely you know that I never travel with any companions, since I'm used to walking alone.'

" 'Hear me out—I know that this traveling companion will just right for you. You will both suit each other quite nicely. You see, the father of the master of this house where I work has also made a vow to visit old Jerusalem. You will get used to each other. He's a local man, of the lower middle class—an elderly man who is kind and actually quite deaf. So it doesn't matter how much you shout at him, he won't hear a thing. If you need to speak with him, you must write it down on paper and then he'll answer. So he will not bother you on the journey, because he won't be talking to you. He hardly speaks even in his own home, but you would be indispensable to him on the journey. His son is providing him with a horse and wagon to get to Odessa, where he will sell both. The old man would like to go on foot, but he needs the horse for his luggage and some packages he is taking to the Lord's tomb, and you could load your knapsack on his wagon. Think about it! How can you let an old, deaf man go off on his own, in a horse-drawn wagon, on such a long journey? We have been looking for some time for a traveling companion for him, but they're all asking too much money. And then it is dangerous to send him off with a stranger, especially since he's carrying money and parcels with him. Do say yes, brother; I assure you it will work out just fine. Agree to do this to the glory of God and for love of your fellowman. I will vouch for you to his family, and they will be overjoyed to hear it. They are kind people and care a great deal for me. I've been working for them for two years already.'

"We had been standing and talking at the entrance to the house. Then he took me inside and introduced me to the master. I realized that this was an honest, decent family, so I agreed to their proposal. We decided to leave, God willing, on the third day after Christmas, right after the Liturgy.

"You see what kinds of coincidences happen in one's life! Yet God and His Divine Providence always guide all our plans and deeds, just as it is written: 'For God is at work in you, both to will and to work for his good pleasure' " [Phil. 2:13].

My spiritual father listened to my story and said, "I rejoice with all my heart, dearest brother, that the Lord has ordained for me to see you again, so soon and so unexpectedly. Since you have some free time on your hands, I will lovingly ask you to stay a bit longer and tell me more about the educational experiences you have encountered on your lengthy pilgrimages. I have listened with such pleasure and delight to all your other stories."

"I will be more than happy to do so," I replied, and I began to talk.

So many things, both good and bad, have happened to me, that it would be impossible to recount them all. Why, I've even forgotten some, for my attention was always more focused on what was guiding and prodding my lazy soul to pray. So I did not spend much time thinking about all the rest—or, rather, I tried to forget the past, as the apostle Paul teaches us, saying: ". . . forgetting what lies behind and striving forward to what lies ahead" [Phil. 3:13]. Even my late starets of blessed memory would tell me that obstacles to the prayer of the heart come from two sources: from the left and from the right. This means that if the enemy fails to prevent us from praying, through vain thoughts and sinful imaginings, then he stirs within us memories of all sorts of edifying things, or he entices us with pleasant thoughts—anything at all—just to lure us away from prayer, which is something unbearable to him.

This is what is called "right-hand theft," and it causes the soul to scorn converse with God and to turn to the pleasure of conversing with its own self or with other creatures. He taught me, therefore, that during prayer I must reject even the most pleasant spiritual thoughts. Moreover, if I should happen to notice during the course of a day that I am spending more time on edifying speculation or conversation than on the essential hidden prayer of the heart, I should consider even this as being immoderate, or as self-seeking spiritual gluttony. This applies especially to beginners, for whom it is vital that the time they spend on prayer must significantly exceed even the time they spend on any other pious activities.

Still, neither can one forget all the rest. It can happen that an experience becomes so ingrained in one's mind that even if one does not think about it often, it remains clearly etched in the memory. A case in point would be the pious family with whom God granted me to spend a few days; I will tell you now about them.

While I was journeying through the Tobolsk province, I happened to be passing through one of the cities of that district. I was down to the last of my dried bread, so I stopped in one of the houses to ask for some. The master of the house said to me, "Thank God that you have come at the right moment! My wife has just taken some fresh bread out of the oven. Here is a warm loaf for you; pray to God for us." I thanked him and started to put the bread in my knapsack when the mistress of the house saw me and said, "Look at your knapsack—it's all worn out! Let me give you another one." And she gave me a good, sturdy one instead. I thanked them with all my heart and went on my way. As I was leaving the city, I stopped in a small shop and asked for some salt. The shopkeeper gave me a small bagful and I rejoiced in my spirit, thanking

The Way of a Pilgrim

God for bringing unworthy me to such good people. Now I would not have to worry about food for a whole week. I could sleep peacefully and be satisfied. Bless the Lord, O my soul!

I had walked about three and a half miles beyond the city when I came across a poor village along that road. There stood a wooden church, simple but nicely decorated with frescoes on the outside. As I walked past it I felt a desire to go inside and worship in this temple of God, so I went on the porch and prayed for a while. Two children, aged five or six, were playing on the grass along the side of the church. I thought they were the priest's children, even though they were extremely well dressed. Still I said my prayers and went on my way. I had walked only ten steps away from the church when I heard shouting behind me: "Dear beggarman! Dear beggarman, wait!" The children, a boy and a girl, had seen me and were running toward me and shouting. I stopped and they ran up to me and each grabbed one of my hands. "Come with us to Mommy—she loves the poor," they said.

"I am not a beggar," I replied. "I'm just a man passing through."

"Then why do you have a knapsack?"

"I keep bread for the road in there. But tell me, where is your mommy?" I asked.

"She's over there, behind the church, just behind that little grove."

They led me into a beautiful garden, in the middle of which stood a large manor house. We went inside, and how neat and clean everything was! The mistress of the house ran out to meet us. "Welcome! Welcome! From where has God sent you to us? Sit down, kind sir, sit down!" She removed the knapsack from my back, put it on the table, and sat me down in one of the softest chairs. "Wouldn't you like something to eat, or some tea? Is there anything at all that you need?"

"I thank you most humbly," I replied, "I have a sack full of food. Although I do drink tea, we peasants are not all that used to it. Your eagerness to help and your affectionate welcome are more precious to me than any refreshments. I will pray to God that He bless you for the biblical spirit of your love of pilgrims." When I had said this I experienced an intense desire to enter into my inner self again. The prayer was kindled in my heart and I needed peace and silence, so I could give reign to this self-kindling flame of prayer and keep others from seeing all the external manifestations that accompany it, such as tears, sighs and the unusual facial gestures and movement of my lips. So I got up and said, "Please excuse me, *Matushka*,* it's time for me to leave. May the Lord Jesus Christ be with you and with your kind little children."

"Oh, no! God forbid that you should leave—I won't let you go! My husband will be coming home from the city this evening. He works there as an appointed

The Way of a Pilgrim

judge, and he'll be so happy to meet you! He considers every pilgrim to be a messenger of God. If you leave now he will be very upset not to have met you. Besides, tomorrow is Sunday and you can pray at the Liturgy with us and then we'll eat together whatever God has provided. We always have guests on each feast day—as many as thirty of Christ's needy brethren. But you have not even told me anything about yourself—where you come from and where you are headed! Stay and talk with me, I love to hear about spiritual matters from devout people. Children, children! Take the pilgrim's knapsack and put it in the chapel—that's where he will spend the night."

I was surprised to hear what she was saying and thought to myself: am I dealing here with a human being, or is she some sort of an apparition?

So I did stay to meet the master of the house. I briefly told him about my journey and that I was headed for Irkutsk.

"Well, then," said the mistress, "you will have to pass through Tobolsk. My mother is a schima nun* now and lives in a women's monastery there. We will give you a letter of introduction and she will receive you. Many people go to her for spiritual counsel. By the way, you can also bring her a book by Saint John of the Ladder, which she asked us to order from Moscow. How nicely all this fits together!"

Finally it was time for dinner, and we all sat down

at the table, where four more ladies joined us. After the first course, one of them got up from the table, bowed to the icon, then to us. She served the second course and sat down again. Then another of the ladies repeated this and served the third course. Observing all this, I asked the mistress of the house, "If I may ask, little mother, are these ladies related to you?"

"Yes, they are sisters to me: this one is the cook, this one is the coachman's wife, that one is the house-keeper, and the last is my maid. They are all mar-ried—I don't have a single unmarried girl in my house."

Having observed and listened to everything, I was even more astonished. I thanked God for bringing me to such devout people and experienced the intense ac-tivity of the prayer in my heart. Since I was eager to be alone so as not to hinder this prayer, I got up from the table and said to the mistress, "No doubt you will need to rest after dinner. I am used to taking a walk, so I will stroll around the garden."

"No," she replied, "I do not need to rest. I will walk with you in the garden, and you will tell me something edifying. If you go alone, the children will pester you. As soon as they see you, they won't leave your side for a moment, because they truly love the needy brethren of Christ and pilgrims."

There was nothing for me to do but go with her. In order to avoid talking about myself when we entered the garden, I bowed to the ground before the mistress and said, "Matushka, in the name of God, please tell me how long you have been living such a devout life and how you achieved such piety."

"Perhaps I should tell you the whole story of my life. You see, my mother is the great-granddaughter of Saint Joasaph, whose relics rest in Belogorod and are open for veneration. We owned a large town house and rented one wing of it to a nobleman, who was not too well off financially. When he died, his widow was pregnant, and then she died after giving birth. My mother had compassion on the poor orphaned child and took him in to raise him. I was born one year later. We grew up together, studied under the same tutors, and became as close as brother and sister. Sometime later my father died, and my mama moved from the city to live right here in the country, on her estate. When we grew up, my mother gave me in marriage to this orphaned young man who had grown up in our house. She settled her entire estate on us and entered a monastery, where she had a cell built for herself. In giving us a mother's blessing, she admonished us to live as Christians, to pray earnestly to God, and above all else to strive to fulfill the most important of God's commandments: to love our neighbors and to feed and help Christ's needy brethren, with simplicity and humility to raise our children in the fear of God, and to treat our servants as brothers. So we have lived here by ourselves these last ten years, trying our best to heed our mother's instructions. We have a guesthouse for the poor, where there are more than ten crippled and needy people in residence at the moment. Perhaps tomorrow we will visit them."

When she had finished her story I asked, "Where is that book by Saint John of the Ladder that you wanted delivered to your mother?"

"Let's go inside and I will find it for you."

No sooner had we sat down to read than the master of the house arrived. Upon seeing me he embraced me warmly, and we exchanged the Christian kiss of peace. Then he took me into his own room and said, "Come, dear brother, to my study and bless my cell. I think that you have had enough of her"—he pointed to his wife. "As soon as she sees a man or woman who is a pilgrim, or someone who is ill, she is more than glad to spend day and night with them. Her entire family has been this way for generations." We went into his study. There were so many books and magnificent icons there, as well as a life-giving crucifix with a life-sized figure of Christ on it and a Bible next to it. I prayed and then said to him: "Sir, what you have here is God's paradise. Here is the Lord Jesus Christ Himself, His most pure Mother, and His holy saints; and these"—I pointed to the books—"are their divinely inspired, living words and teachings, which can never be silenced. I would expect that you enjoy frequent spiritual converse with them."

"Yes, I admit it," said the master. "I do love to read."

"What sort of books do you have here?" I asked.

"I have many spiritual books," he replied. "Here is the *Chet'-Minei** for the entire year, the works of Saint John Chrysostom and Saint Basil the Great. There are many theological and philosophical works, as well as collections of many sermons of the most recent and celebrated preachers. My library is worth five thousand rubles."

"By any chance, would you have a book about prayer?" I asked.

"I love to read about prayer. Here is the most recent work on that subject, written by a priest in Saint Petersburg." He reached for a volume on the Lord's Prayer, the Our Father, and we began to read it with pleasure.

A short time later, the mistress of the house brought us some tea, while the children brought in a large silver basket filled with some sort of biscuits or pastries that I had never before eaten. The husband took the book from me, gave it to his wife, and said, "Since she reads so beautifully, we will make her read to us while we take some refreshment." She started reading and we listened. As I listened to her, I was able simultaneously to attend to the prayer in my heart. The more she read, the stronger the prayer became and filled me with delight. Suddenly, it seemed to me as if someone passed before my eyes in a flash, through the air—as if it were my late starets. I shuddered, but not wanting them to notice this, I quickly said, "Forgive me, I must have dozed off." At that moment I felt as if the starets's spirit had penetrated my own spirit, as if he had illumined it. I experienced a certain enlightenment in my understanding, and a multitude of thoughts about prayer came to me. I had just made the sign of the cross over myself in an attempt to banish these thoughts when the mistress finished reading the book and her husband asked me if I had enjoyed it. So we started a discussion on it.

"I liked it very much," I replied. "The Lord's Prayer, the Our Father, is more exalted and more precious than all the recorded prayers we Christians have, for it was given to us by the Lord Jesus Christ Himself. The commentary on it was very good, except that it focuses primarily on Christian works. In my reading of the holy Fathers, I have read also the contemplative, mystical commentaries on this prayer."

"In which of the Fathers did you read this?"

"Well, for example, in Saint Maximus the Confessor and, in the *Philokalia*, in Saint Peter of Damascus."

"Do you remember anything you read? Please, tell us about it!"

"Why, of course! Let's take the first words of the prayer: *Our Father, Who art in heaven.* In the book we read today the interpretation of these words is to be understood as a call to brotherly love for one's neighbors, as being all children of the one Father. This is true, but the Fathers explain this further, on a deeper spiritual level. They say that the words of this maxim are a call to raise the mind to heaven, to the heavenly Father, and to remember our obligation to place ourselves and live our lives in the presence of God at each and every moment. The words *hallowed be Thy Name* are explained in your book as being a sign of reverence, so that the Name of God would never be uttered disrespectfully or taken in false oaths. In a word, the holy Name of God must be spoken reverently and not taken in vain. The mystical commentators see these words as a direct request for the gift of interior prayer of the heart—a request that the most holy Name of God be engraved upon the heart and hallowed by the self-acting prayer, so that it might sanctify all our feelings and spiritual powers.

"The words *Thy Kingdom come* are explained by mystical commentators in the following way: may inner peace, tranquillity, and spiritual joy come into our hearts. Your book explains the words *give us this day our daily bread* as a request for the material needs of our bodies—not in excess, but enough to fill our own needs and to help the needy. However, Saint Maximus the Confessor interprets *daily bread* to mean the feeding of the soul with heavenly bread—the Word of God—and the union of the soul with God, through constant remembrance of Him and through the unceasing interior prayer of the heart."

"Ah! That is a great deed, but it is almost impossible for those who live in the world to attain to interior prayer!" exclaimed the master of the house. "We're lucky when the Lord helps us simply to say our prayers without laziness!"

"Don't look at it that way, Batyushka. If it were so impossible and overwhelmingly difficult, then God would not have admonished us all to do it. His strength is made perfect also in weakness. From their own experience the Fathers offer us ways and methods that make it easier for us to attain to the prayer of the heart. Of course, for hermits they teach special and more advanced methods, but they also prescribe convenient methods that faithfully guide lay people to attain to the prayer of the heart."

"I have never come across anything as detailed as this in my reading," said the master.

"Please, if you would like me to, I will read to you from the *Philokalia*."

I went to get my *Philokalia*, found the article by Saint Peter of Damascus in section 3, and read the following: " 'More important than attending to breathing, one must learn to call upon the Name of God at all times, in all places, and during all manner of activity. The apostle says: *pray without ceasing;* that is, he teaches constant remembrance of God at all times, in all places, and under any circumstances. If you are busy doing something, you must remember the Creator of all things; if you see light, remember Him who gave it to you. If you look at the sky, the earth, the waters and all that is in them, marvel and glorify the Creator of all. If you are putting your clothes on, remember Him Whose gift they are and thank Him Who provides everything in your life. In short, let every action be an occasion for you always to remember and praise God. And before you know it, you are praying unceasingly and your soul will always rejoice in this.' Do you see now how this method for achieving unceasing prayer is convenient, easy, and accessible to any person who has at least some measure of human feelings?"

They were very impressed by all this. The master embraced me with delight and thanked me. Then he looked through my Philokalia and said, "I will order this from Petersburg as soon as I can. For now I will copy this passage so I don't forget it. Read it to me again." He wrote it down quickly and neatly. Then he exclaimed, "My God! Why, I even have an icon of the holy Damascene!" (It was probably one of Saint John of Damascus.) He picked up a picture frame, inserted the handwritten sheet behind the glass, and hung it beneath the icon. "There," he said, "the living word of God's saint, hanging right under his image. It will serve to remind me always to put his redemptive advice into practice."

After this we sat down to dinner, and the same people as before sat with us, men and women. What reverent silence and peace there were at the dinner table! After the meal we all, adults and children, spent a long time in prayer. I was asked to chant the Akathist to the Most Sweet Jesus.

After prayers the servants went to bed, while the three of us remained in the room. The mistress brought me a white shirt and socks. I bowed to the ground before her and said, "Matushka, I will not take the socks, for I have never worn them in my life. We peasants are used to always wearing *onoochi**. She hurried out of the room and brought back her old robe, made of thin yellow fabric, and ripped it in half to make two onoochi. "Look," said the master, "the poor man's footwear is falling apart." He brought a pair of his own *bashmaki** that were new and in a large size, the kind that were worn over boots. "Go in that empty room and change your clothes," he said. I did so, and when I returned they made me sit down and began to change my shoes. The husband started to wrap the onoochi around my feet, while his wife pulled the bashmaki on top of them. At first I protested, but they insisted, saying, "Sit and be quiet—Christ washed the feet of His apostles." There was nothing else I could do, so I burst into tears and they wept with me. Afterward, the mistress retired for the night with the children, while the master and I went to the summerhouse in the garden.

For a long time we did not feel sleepy, so we lay awake and talked. Then he began to ply me with questions: "Now tell me the truth, in God's name and on your conscience. Who are you? You must come from a good family and have chosen willingly to become a fool for Christ.* You write and read very well; you speak correctly and are able to think and discuss things properly. These things could not have been learned from a peasant upbringing."

"I spoke the honest truth, from the sincerity of my heart, when I told you and your wife about my background. I never thought to lie or deceive you. Why would I do that? Everything I have shared with you is not my own, but what I learned from my late starets, who was filled with divine wisdom, and what I carefully read in the holy Fathers. My ignorance has been enlightened most of all by interior prayer, which I did not acquire on my on. It came to life in my heart through God's mercy and the guidance of my starets. But this is something that is possible for each man. All it takes is to descend silently into one's heart and call more frequently on the enlightening name of Jesus Chirst, and immediately one will experience inner illumination. Then all things will be revealed to the understanding and one will comprehend even certain mysteries of the Kingdom of God through such enlightenment. Even to know that one can plumb the depths of one's own being, see one's inner self, be delighted by this self-knowledge, experience warm tenderness and shed tears over one's fallen state and distorted will, is already a deep and enlightened mystery. It is possible, and not all that difficult, to discuss and converse wisely with people, for the mind and heart existed before any human learning or human wisdom was acquired. If one has a mind, it can be educated, either by science or by experience; but where there is no understanding, then no amount of discipline will help. The fact is that we are far removed from our own real self, and we have little desire to confront that self. Instead, we run from any encounter with our real self, choosing aimless trifles over the truth. Then we try to convince ourselves that we'd be more than glad to live the spiritual life and take up praying, but there's never enough time for it, because all the cares and worries of our lives take up all our time. And yet, what is more important: the redemptive eternal life of the soul, or the short-lived life of the body, which we spend so much time attending to? It is this, which I spoke of, that leads people either to good judgment or to stupidity."

"Forgive me, dear brother, I did not question you merely from curiosity, but from a kindhearted sense of

Christian empathy, and also because two years ago I had an experience that now prompted my question. You see, a beggar with a military discharge passport came to us. He was old, decrepit, and so poor that he barely had any clothes or shoes on him. He spoke little and so simply that one took him for a peasant from the steppes. We took him into the guesthouse for the poor, and some five days later he became so ill that we moved him into this summerhouse, and my wife and I began to nurse and care for him. Finally it became clear that he was close to dying, so we prepared him by calling our priest to come and hear his confession, to give him Communion, and to administer the sacrament of Holy Unction. The day before he died he got out of bed, asked for a pen and a sheet of paper, and requested that his door be locked and no one allowed inside while he wrote his last will and testament to his son. He asked also that after his death we mail it to the address he would provide in Saint Petersburg. I was astounded to see that not only did he write a beautiful and exceedingly cultured hand, but the composition was excellent; it was grammatically correct and very gentle in style. Tomorrow I will read his will to you—I kept a copy of it. All this surprised me and made me curious enough to ask him about his background and life. He made me vow that I would not reveal anything while he was still alive, and then, to the glory of God, he told me the story of his life.

" 'I was a very wealthy prince, living an opulent and dissipated life of great luxury. My wife died and I lived alone with my son, who was fortunate to be serving as a captain in the Guards. One day we were preparing to go to a ball at an important person's house when I became furious with my valet. Unable to control my temper, I hit him very hard on the head and ordered him sent back to his village. This happened in the evening, and the next day the valet died from an inflammation on his brain. Yet I was not bothered too much by this. I regretted my rash behavior but soon forgot about the incident. Six weeks later the dead valet began to appear to me, at first in my dreams. He hounded me every night, reproaching me and continually repeating, "Unscrupulous man! You are my murderer!" Then I also began to see him when I was fully awake. The longer this went on, the more frequently he would appear to me, until he was hounding me almost continuously. Finally I began to see not only him but also other dead men whom I had sorely offended, and even women whom I had seduced. They all continuously reproached me, robbing me of all my peace until I could no longer sleep or eat or do anything at all. I became so utterly exhausted that my skin stuck to my very bones. No matter what cures they attempted, not even the most experienced doctors could help me. I went abroad to try new cures, but after six months my condition had not improved in the least. The tormenting apparitions mercilessly grew worse and worse, and I was brought home barely alive. Indeed, my soul experienced the fullest measure of the torments of hell, before it had even left my body. It was then that I was convinced of the existence of hell and what it is really like.

" 'In this tormented state I acknowledged my sins, repented, confessed, and set free all my servants. I vowed that for the rest of my life I would inflict all manner of toil and hardship upon myself and humble myself in poverty, so that because of my sins I would become the lowest servant to people of the lowest class. As soon as I had firmly resolved to do this, all the tormenting apparitions vanished. I cannot fully describe the joy and delight that I experienced from having made my peace with God, and it was this experience that taught me what paradise is and how the Kingdom of God is revealed in our hearts. Soon I was completely cured and set out to fulfill my vow. I obtained a military discharge passport and, without telling anyone, I left my native land. It is now fifteen years since I have been wandering through Siberia. Sometimes I would hire myself out to peasants, to do whatever work I was capable of, and other times I would beg for food in the name of Christ. Ah, but in spite of all my poverty I knew such bliss, happiness, and peace of conscience! This can be fully experienced only by someone who has been brought from the torments of hell into God's Kingdom, by the mercy of the holy Intercessor.'

"When he finished telling me all this, he gave me his will to mail to his son, and the next day he died. I have kept a copy of it in my briefcase, tucked inside my Bible. If you would like to read it, I'll get it for you. Here it is!"

I unfolded it and read the following:

In the name of God, glorified in the Trinity, the Father and the Son and the Holy Spirit.

My dearest son!

It has been fifteen years since you last saw your father. Although you have not had any news of him, from time to time he has managed to hear about you and has cherished a father's love for you. That love compels me to send to you these last words from my deathbed, with the hope that they will serve as a lesson in your life.

You know how I suffered for my carelessness and my thoughtless life; but you do not know of the bliss I experienced during the years of my anonymous pilgrimage and how I delighted in the fruits of repentance.

I die in peace in the home of one who has been a kind benefactor to me and also to you, for the blessings poured out upon the father must also touch the sensitive son. Express to him my gratitude in whatever way you can.

I leave you with my paternal blessing and adjure you always to remember God, to guard your conscience, and to be prudent, kind, and discerning.

Treat your subordinates as favorably and kindly as you can, and do not scorn the poor and homeless, remembering that your dying father found peace and tranquillity for his tormented soul only in poverty and pilgrimage.

Beseeching God's blessings on you, I peacefully close my eyes in the hope of eternal life, through the mercy of mankind's Intercessor, Jesus Christ.

Your father . . .

Thus the kind master and I lay in the summerhouse and chatted. Then I asked him, "I would think, Batyushka, that keeping a guesthouse for the poor brings you its own worries and problems. There are quite a few of our fellow pilgrims who wander because they have nothing better to do or because they are too lazy to work. Sometimes they even cause trouble on the road, as I have had occasion to see for myself."

"We have not had too many such cases," he replied. "Mostly they have been genuine pilgrims. Yet we tend to welcome the troublemakers even more and urge them to stay longer with us. By living among our kind beggars, among the brethren of Christ, they are often reformed and leave the guesthouse as meek and humble people. We had a case like this just recently. One of our local middle-class townsmen became so depraved that everyone began to chase him from their doorsteps with sticks. No one would give him so much as a piece of bread. He was a violent, pugnacious drunk and he even stole. He came to us in this condition, quite starved, and asked for some bread and wine, the latter being what he was extremely eager for. We welcomed him kindly and said, 'Live with us and we will give you as much wine as you want, but only under the condition that when you get drunk, you will go immediately to bed and sleep it off. Should you create the slightest disturbance or trouble, we will not only throw you out and never let you come back here, but I will even report you to the magistrate or the town governor and have you sent to a penal colony for suspicious vagrancy.' He agreed to all this and came to live with us. For a week or more he really did drink a great deal, as much as he wanted. Yet he always kept his promise and went to bed, because he was too addicted to wine (and could not risk being deprived of it). Or else he would go into the garden and quietly lie down there. When he was sober, his fellow beggars tried to urge him to stop drinking, or at least to start by cutting down. Gradually he began to drink less and less, until finally, some three months later, he was completely dry. He has a job somewhere now and no longer needs to beg for his bread. Why, just the day before yesterday he came over to thank me."

What wisdom, I thought, has been wrought under the guidance of love, and I exclaimed, "Blessed be God, Who has revealed His mercy in the household that is under your care!"

After this conversation the master and I slept for

about an hour, or an hour and a half, until we heard the bell for matins. We got up and went to church. Just as we walked inside we saw the mistress, who had been there for some time already with the children. We stood through matins and then the Divine Liturgy, which followed soon after. The master and I stood with the little boy in the altar, while his wife and daughter stood near the altar window so they could observe the elevation of the Gifts. My God! How they prayed as they knelt, with tears of joy streaming down their faces! Their faces were so radiant that just watching them brought forth the fullness of my own tears.

After the Liturgy the gentlefolk, the priest, the servants, and all the beggars went to the dining room to eat. There were some forty beggars, and everyone—the crippled, the infirm, the children—all sat down at one table. What silence and tranquillity there was! Drawing on my boldness, I quietly said to the master, "In monasteries they read from the lives of the saints during meals. You could do the same, since you have the complete text." He turned to his wife and said, "Actually, Masha, why don't we start doing that regularly? It would be most edifying. I will read first, at this meal, then you will read at the next one, and then Batyushka can read. After that, whoever else knows how to read may take turns."

The priest, who was eating, said, "I love to listen, but as for reading, well, with all due respect, I do not have the time for it. The minute I get home I have so much to do, so many duties and concerns to attend to, I hardly know where to begin. First one thing needs to be done, then another; then there are all the children and the cows need to be let out. My days are so completely taken up with all this that I'm not up to reading or studying. I've long since forgotten even what I learned at seminary." When I heard this I shuddered, but the mistress, who was sitting next to me, grasped my hand and said, "Father speaks this way from humility. He always humbles himself, but he is righteous and the kindest of men. He has been a widower for twenty years now and has been raising a whole family of grandchildren, as well as serving frequent services in church." Her words reminded me of the following saying of Nikitas Stethatos in the *Philokalia:* "The nature of things is measured by the interior disposition of the soul; that is, the kind of person one is will determine what he thinks of others." He goes on to say: "He who has attained to genuine prayer and love no longer puts things into categories. He does not separate the righteous from the sinners, but loves all equally and does not judge them, just as God gives the sun to shine and the rain to fall both on the just and the unjust."

This was followed again by silence. A completely blind beggar from the guesthouse sat across from me.

The master fed him, cutting up the fish and handing him a spoon filled with broth.

Observing him closely, I noticed that the beggar's mouth was constantly open and his tongue kept moving about inside, as if it were trembling. This made me think that perhaps he was a man of prayer, so I continued to watch him. At the end of the meal one of the old women suddenly became so ill that she began to moan. The master and his wife took her into their bedroom and lay her down on the bed. The wife stayed to watch over her, while the priest went to get the Presanctified Gifts,* just to be on the safe side. The master ordered his carriage and went to fetch the doctor, while the rest of us departed.

I felt a kind of prayerful inner quiet, a strong need to pour my soul out in prayer, and it had already been forty-eight hours since I had experienced any silence or solitude. It felt as if a flood were building up in my heart that strained to burst forth and spill out into all my limbs. Since I was struggling to contain it, I felt a soreness in my heart, albeit a pleasurable one, that insistently demanded the peace of silence and could be satisfied only by prayer. Through this it was revealed to me why people who had attained to genuine self-acting interior prayer fled the company of others and took refuge in anonymous solitude. I understood also why the venerable Hesychios said that even the most beneficial conversation was idle chatter when taken to excess, just as Saint Ephraim the Syrian said, "Good speech is silver, but silence is pure gold."

As I considered all this, I walked to the guesthouse, where everyone was resting after the meal. I climbed up into the attic, calmed down, rested, and prayed a bit. When the beggars had arisen from their rest, I found the blind man and walked with him just beyond the kitchen garden, where we sat down alone and began to talk.

"For God's sake, would you tell me if you are praying the Jesus prayer for spiritual benefit?"

"I have been praying it unceasingly for a long time now."

"And what is it that you experience from it?"

"Only that I cannot be without the prayer day or night."

"How did God reveal this practice to you? Tell me everything, dear brother."

"Well, you see, I once belonged to a local guild and earned my living as a tailor. I traveled to other provinces and villages, making clothing for the peasants.

"One time I happened to spend a longer time in one of the villages, living with a peasant for whose family I was making clothing. On one of the feast days I noticed three books lying near the icon case, and I asked, 'Who in the household knows how to read?' 'No one,' they replied. 'These books were left to us by our uncle, who knew how to read and write.' I picked up one of the books and opened it at random. On one of the pages I happened to read the following, which I still remember to this day: 'Unceasing prayer is calling always upon the Name of God, whether one is conversing or sitting down, walking, working, or eating, or occupied with any other activity—in all places and at all times one should call upon the Name of God.' After reading this I began to realize that it would be quite convenient for me to do this. So I began to repeat the prayer in a quiet whisper while I sewed and found it much to my liking. The others living with me in the hut noticed this and began to make fun of me. 'What are you, some sort of wizard?' they asked. 'What are you whispering all the time? Are you weaving some sort of spell?' So to cover up what I was doing, I stopped moving my lips and began to pray only with my tongue. Eventually, I grew so accustomed to the prayer that day and night my tongue would form the words on its own, and this became quite pleasant for me.

"So I lived this way for quite a while, going from village to village to sew, until all of a sudden I became completely blind. Almost everyone in our family suffers from 'dark water.'* When I became poverty-stricken, our guild placed me in an almshouse in Tobolsk, the capital of our province. I was on my way there when the master and mistress urged me to stop over here so they could provide me with a cart that would take me to Tobolsk."

"What was the name of the book you read? Was it by any chance the *Philokalia*?"

"Honestly, I do not know; I didn't even look at the title."

I brought my *Philokalia* to him and in part 4 I found the passage by Patriarch Callistus, which the blind man had just quoted from memory. I read it back to him and he cried out, "That's it, that's exactly it! Keep on reading, brother—this is just wonderful!"

When I got to the line "One should pray with the heart," he began to ply me with questions: "What does this mean?" and "How do you do this?" I told him that all the teachings on the prayer of the heart were provided in detail in this book, the *Philokalia*. He earnestly beseeched me to read the whole thing to him.

"I'll tell you what we'll do," I said. "When are you leaving for Tobolsk?"

"I could leave this very moment," he replied.

"Then let's do this: since I am thinking also of heading out tomorrow, we can travel together and I can read to you everything concerning the prayer of the heart. I'll also explain how to locate the place of the heart and how to enter into it."

"But what about the cart?" he asked.

"Eh, who needs a cart? As if we don't know how far Tobolsk is! It's only about a hundred miles, and we'll walk slowly. Think how good it will be for the two of us alone to travel together. It will be much easier for us to talk and read about prayer as we walk." So we agreed on this.

That evening the master himself came to call us to dinner. After the meal we informed him that the blind man and I would be traveling together and that we did not need the cart, since it would be easier this way for us to read the *Philokalia.* When he heard this, the master said, "I too enjoyed the *Philokalia.* In fact, I've already written a letter, enclosing some money, which I'll mail to Saint Petersburg on my way to the court-house tomorrow. I've asked them to send it to me at the very first return of post."

The next day we set off, after warmly thanking our hosts for their most exemplary love and hospitality. They both accompanied us for over half a mile from their house. Thus it was that we took our leave of them.

The blind man and I walked short distances at a time, some six to ten miles a day. The rest of the time we sat in secluded spots and read from the *Philokalia.* I read to him all that there was on the prayer of the heart, following the order that my late starets had indicated to me, beginning with the book of Nicephorus the Solitary, Saint Gregory of Sinai, and so on. How greedily and attentively he took in everything and how it pleased and delighted him! Then he began to ask me such questions about prayer that my mind was not equal to answering them. When we had read all the necessary passages from the *Philokalia*, he earnestly beseeched me actually to show him how the mind can find the heart, how to bring the Name of Jesus Christ into it, and how to experience the delightful interior prayer of the heart. I explained the following to him: "You are blind and can see nothing, but are you not able to visualize in your mind that which you once could see with your eyes—a person or some object or one of your limbs, such as a hand or a foot? Are you not able to visualize it as vividly as if you were actually looking at it and to concentrate and focus even your blind eyes on it?"

"I can do that," said the blind man.

"Well, then, do the same thing and try to visualize your heart with your mind. Focus your eyes as if you were looking at it, right through the wall of your chest cavity. Try to visualize it as vividly as possible in your mind, and with your ears listen to the steady rhythm of its beating. When you have succeeded with this, then begin to repeat the words of the prayer, in accompaniment to each beat of your heart, keeping your eyes focused on it all the while. Thus with the first beat you will say, verbally or mentally, the word *Lord;* with the second, *Jesus;* with the third, *Christ;* with the fourth, *have mercy;* with the fifth, *on me.* Repeat this over and over again. It should be easy for you, since you have already learned the basics of the prayer of the heart.

Eventually, when you get used to it, then you can begin to repeat the full Jesus prayer in your heart, in time with a steady rhythm of inhaling and exhaling, as the Fathers taught. As you inhale, you visualize your heart and say, 'Lord Jesus Christ.' As you exhale, you say, 'have mercy on me!' Do this as much and as often as you can, and soon you will experience a delicate but pleasant soreness in your heart, which will be followed by warmth and a warming tenderness in your heart. If you do this, with God's help you will attain to the delightful self-acting interior prayer of the heart. However, as you do all this, guard against mental imaginings and any sort of visions. Reject everything your imagination produces, for the holy Fathers strictly teach that interior prayer must be a visionless exercise, lest one fall into delusion."

The blind man listened attentively to everything and then earnestly began to practice the specified method of prayer. He would spend an especially long time on it at night when we stopped to rest. After about five days he began to feel an intense warmth and an indescribably pleasant sensation in his heart, along with a great desire to devote himself continually to this prayer, which was stirring in him a love for Jesus Christ. From time to time he would begin to see a light, though he discerned no visible things or objects in it. At times, when he entered into his heart, it seemed to him that a strong flame, like that of a burning candle, would flare up delightfully within his heart and would illuminate him as it rushed up and outward through his throat. This light made it possible for him to see things even at a great distance, which did occur on one occasion.

We happened to be walking through a forest, and he was fully and silently absorbed in his prayer. Suddenly he said to me, "What a pity! The church is already burning, and there—the belfry has collapsed."

"Stop imagining things," I said. "That's nothing but a temptation. You must quickly banish all thoughts. How can you possibly see what's happening in the city when we're still almost eight miles away from it?"

He took my advice, continued praying, and was silent. Toward evening we arrived in the ctiy, and I actually saw several burned-down buildings and a collapsed belfry, which had stood on wooden piles. Many people were milling about, amazed that the belfry had not crushed anyone when it collapsed. I estimated that this tragedy had occurred exactly at the time the blind man had told me about it. So he began saying to me, "You said I was imagining things, and yet it happened just as I described it. How can one not love and be grateful to the Lord Jesus Christ, Who manifests His grace to sinners, to the blind and the unwise! I thank you too for teaching me the work of the heart."

"You can love Jesus Christ and be as grateful to

Him as you will," I said, "but beware of accepting visions as direct revelations of grace, because such things can often occur as natural manifestations, according to the natural order of things. Man's soul is not absolutely bound by space and matter. It can also see events through darkness and at very great distances, as if they were happening nearby. It is we who do not give power and momentum to this capability in our souls, and we squelch it beneath the bonds of either the carnal fleshiness of our bodies or our confused thoughts and scattered ideas. Yet, when we focus our attention on the inner self, divert our concentration from everything external, and refine our mind, then the soul finds its truest fulfillment and exercises its highest powers, which is quite natural. I heard from my late starets that nonpraying people or people who have a certain ability or suffer from sick disorders are able to see, in the darkest room, the aura of light that radiates from all things, to distinguish between various objects, to sense the presence of their double, and to know the thoughts of others. But what occurs during the prayer of the heart is the direct result of God's grace, and it is so delightful that no tongue can describe it, attribute it to anything material, or compare it to anything at all. All physical sensations are base in comparison to the delightful experience of grace acting within the heart."

My blind man listened seriously to all this and was

even more humbled by it. The prayer continued to increase within his heart, delighting him beyond description. I rejoiced in this with all my heart and earnestly thanked God for granting me to have met such a blessed servant of His.

At last we arrived in Tobolsk, where I took him to the almshouse. After kindly parting with him, I left him there and continued on my own journey.

For a month I walked slowly, reflecting in depth on how edifying and encouraging the good experiences in life can be. I read the *Philokalia* frequently to verify all that I had told the blind man of prayer. The edifying example of his experience kindled in me a zeal, gratitude, and love for the Lord. The prayer of the heart delighted me so much that I thought there could be no one happier than I in the whole world and could not imagine how there could be any greater or deeper contentment in the Kingdom of Heaven. Not only did I experience all this within my soul, but everything around me appeared to be enchanting and inspired me with love for and gratitude to God. People, trees, plants, and animals—I felt kinship with them all and discovered how each bore the seal of the Name of Jesus Christ. At times I felt so lightweight, as if I had no body and were not walking but rather joyously floating through the air. At other times I entered so fully into myself that I saw clearly all my inner organs, and this caused me to marvel at the wisdom that went into creating the human body. Sometimes I knew such joy that I felt as if I had been crowned a king. It was at such moments of consolation that I wished that God would grant me to die as soon as possible, so that I could pour myself out in gratitude at His feet in the spiritual world.

Yet it became apparent to me that my enjoyment of these experiences was tempered or had been regulated by God's will, because I soon began to experience some sort of anxiety and fear in my heart. "I hope this is not another sign of some upcoming disaster or misfortune," I thought, "such as that incident with the village girl to whom I taught the Jesus prayer in the chapel!" Clouds of thoughts descended upon my mind, and I remembered the words of the blessed John of Karpathos, who said that often the teacher submits to humiliation and suffers misfortune and temptations for those who will benefit from him spiritually. After struggling for a while with such thoughts, I began to pray more earnestly, and this banished them completely. I was encouraged by this and said to myself, "God's will be done! Anything that Jesus Christ may send my way I am ready to endure for my wretchedness and arrogant disposition—for even those to whom I had recently disclosed the secret of entering the heart and of interior prayer had been prepared directly by God's hidden guidance, before I met them." This thought calmed me, and once again I set off with consolation and with the prayer, feeling more joyous than I had been before.

It rained for about two days and the road had completely turned to mud, so that my legs sank into it and I was barely able to walk. So I walked through the steppe and thus did not come across any human habitation for almost ten miles. At last, one day toward evening, I came upon a farmstead right near the road. I was overjoyed and thought to myself, "I can ask to spend the night and rest up here, and I'll accept whatever God sends my way tomorrow morning. Perhaps even the weather will be better."

As I approached I saw a drunk old man wearing a military overcoat and sitting on a mound of earth by the farmhouse. I bowed to him and said, "Would it be possible to ask someone if I could spend the night here?"

"Who else could let you do that but me?" the old man bellowed. "I'm in charge here! This is a post office and I'm the postmaster."

"Well, then, Batyushka, will you permit me to spend the night here?"

"Do you have a passport? Let's see some legal proof of who you are!"

I gave him my passport, and he had it in his hands when he asked, "Well, where's the passport?"

"You're holding it in your hands," I replied.

"Oh, well, then—let's go inside the hut."

The postmaster put on his glasses, studied the passport, and said, "It's a legal document, all right. You can stay the night. I'm a good man, you know. Here— I'll even offer you a welcome drink."

"I've never had a drink in my entire life," I replied.

"Well, who cares! At least have dinner with us."

"I sat down to table with him and his cook, a young peasant woman who had already had one too many herself. They sat me down to eat with them, and during the entire meal they quarreled, scolding each other. By the end of the meal they were well into a fight. Then the postmaster went off to sleep in the pantry, while the cook began clearing the table, washing the cups and spoons and cursing her old man.

I sat for a while and decided it would be some time before she calmed down, so I said, "Matushka, where could I sleep for the night? I'm exhausted from my journey."

"Here, Batyushka, I'll make you up a bed." She pulled another bench up to the one near the front window, covered it with a felt blanket, and put a pillow at the head of it. I lay down and shut my eyes to make it look as if I were sleeping. The cook continued to putter around for a long time until at last she had cleaned up. She doused the fire and had started coming over to me when suddenly the entire window in the front corner of the house—the frame, the glass, and splinters from the lintel—came showering down with a frightful crash. The entire hut shook, and from just outside the window there came a sickening groan, shouting, and loud scuffling noises. The peasant woman sprang back in terror and jumped into the middle of the room, where she went crashing down on the floor. I jumped up half conscious, thinking that the very ground under me had split wide open. Then I saw two coach drivers entering the hut. They carried between them a man so covered with blood that you couldn't even see his face, which horrified me even more. He was a royal courier who had been on his way here for a change of horses. His coach driver had miscalculated the turn into the gates, the carriage pole had knocked out the window, and, as there was a ditch in front of the house, the wagon had overturned. The courier was thrown clear, and he deeply gouged his head against a sharp stake in the ground that was propping up the earthern mound that served as a bench. He demanded some water and wine to wash his wound with, and after bathing it with some of the wine, he drank a glass of it himself. Then he shouted, "Get the horses!" I went over to him and said: "Batyushka, how can you travel when you're in such pain?"

"A royal courier has no time to be sick," he replied and galloped away. The coach drivers dragged the unconscious peasant woman to the stove in the corner of the room and covered her with a bast hearth rug.

"She's only in shock from being so frightened.

She'll come out of it." The postmaster had another drink to ease his hangover and went back to bed, leaving me all alone.

Soon the peasant woman got up and began to pace back and forth, from one corner of the room to the other, until finally she walked out of the hut. I said my prayers and realized how exhausted I was; but I did manage to catch some sleep just before dawn.

In the morning I took my leave of the postmaster and set off. As I walked I offered up my prayer with faith, hope, and gratitude to the Father of all blessings and consolations, Who had delivered me from an impending disaster.

Six years after this incident I was passing a women's monastery and stopped in their church to pray. The abbess was most hospitable to pilgrims and invited me inside after the Liturgy, asking that some tea be brought to me. Then some unexpected guests arrived for the abbess, and she went to greet them, leaving me alone with her nuns. The one who started to pour my tea struck me as a truly humble woman, so I could not resist asking her, "Matyushka, have you been in this monastery a long time?"

"Five years," she replied. "I was out of my mind when they brought me here. God was merciful to me and the mother abbess let me stay and take the veil."

"What caused you to go out of your mind?" I asked.

"I was in shock from a terrifying experience that

happened while I was working at a post office. It was at night and I was sleeping when some horses knocked out one of the windows, and I went mad from fear. For an entire year my family took me from one shrine to another, and it was only here that I was healed." Upon hearing this my soul rejoiced and glorified God, Who so wisely orders all things for the good.

"There were also many other incidents," I said, turning to my spiritual father. "Were I to relate them all, in the order they occurred, three days and nights would not suffice to tell it all. However, I will tell you about one more incident."

One clear summer day, near the road I saw a cemetery, or what one would call a churchyard, a church, with nothing but houses for the clergy. The call to Liturgy sounded, and I started walking to the church. Some local people were also headed in that direction, while others sat on the grass not far from the church. When they saw me hurrying along, they said, "Don't hurry, there's time enough to stand around before the service starts. The services here are very long, because the priest is in poor health and he drags them out." Indeed, the service was very long. The priest was a young man, but frightfully thin and pale. He celebrated and moved about very slowly, yet with great devotion. At the end of the service, with great depth of feeling he gave an excellent and intelligible sermon on the various ways one can acquire a love for God.

The priest invited me to his home and asked me to stay for lunch. Sitting at table, I said to him, "How devoutly and slowly you serve, Batyushka!"

"Yes," he replied, "even though the parishioners don't like it and grumble. But what can one do? I love to reflect on every word of a prayer and to relish it, for each word that is pronounced without an inner experience and appreciation of it brings no benefit either to one's own self or to others. It all boils down to the interior life and recollected prayer! And yet," he continued, "how few concern themselves with the interior life! This is because people do not want to do it, because they do not care about inner spiritual enlightenment," said the priest.

"But how is one to acquire it?" I asked again. "It would seem to require such depths of wisdom."

"Quite a bit. In order to be spiritually enlightened and to live a recollected interior life, one must take any single passage from the Holy Scriptures, focus all one's attention and meditate on it, for as long as possible, and the light of understanding will be revealed. The same must happen with prayer: if you want it to be pure, correct, and delightful, then you must choose any brief prayer, consisting of a few but powerful words. Repeat it frequently, for long periods of time, and then you will acquire a taste for praying."

The priest's advice pleased me. How practical and simple it was, and yet how deep and wise! In my mind

I thanked God for having led me to such a true shepherd of His church.

When the meal was over, the priest said to me, "Why don't you take a nap after dinner while I read the Bible and prepare tomorrow's sermon." So I went to the kitchen, which was empty except for an extremely old woman who sat alone in the corner, hunched over and coughing. I sat down near the window, took the *Philokalia* out of my bag, and began to read quietly to myself. After a while I happened to hear that the old woman in the corner was whispering the unceasing Jesus prayer. I rejoiced to hear this continuous repetition of the Lord's most holy Name, so I said to her, "How good it is, Matushka, that you pray unceasingly! It is the best thing a Christian can do for his salvation."

"Yes, Batyushka," she replied, "at my old age the only joy for me is to ask the Lord's forgiveness."

"How long has it been since you have made such a habit of this prayer?"

"Since I was a little girl, Batyushka. I couldn't live without it, for the Jesus prayer saved me from ruin and death."

"How is that? Please tell me about it, to the glory of God and in praise of the blessed power of the Jesus prayer." I put the *Philokalia* back in my bag and moved closer to the old woman, and she began to speak.

"I was a young, good-looking girl. My parents arranged to give me in marriage, and the very day before the wedding my bridegroom was coming to see us. On his way over, about ten steps from the house, he suddenly collapsed and died without even a gasp! I was so frightened by this that I refused ever to marry and decided to lead a celibate life, visiting shrines and praying to God. However, because I was so young I was afraid to travel alone, lest I be molested by evil people. Then an old woman I knew, who was a pilgrim, advised me that whatever road I happened to be walking on I should unceasingly repeat the Jesus prayer. She solemnly promised me that no harm could come to me on my journey while I repeated this prayer. I believed this and, indeed, everything went well, even when I traveled to distant shrines. My parents gave me money for these trips.

"As I grew old, I became infirm and this priest was kind enough to feed me and let me stay here."

I listened to her with such delight, not knowing how to thank God for a day so full of such edifying lessons. Then I asked the kind and devout priest for his blessing and, rejoicing, I set off again on my own journey.

Then again, not too long ago, as I was on my way here I passed through the Kazansk district and had another experience that taught me how clearly and vitally the power of praying in the name of Jesus Christ is revealed, even in those who practice it without a conscious awareness of doing so, and how the frequency and duration of repeating it is the surest and quickest way to acquiring the fruits of this prayer. It happened once that I spent the night in a Tatar village. On entering it I saw a carriage and a Russian coachman standing next to the window of one of the huts. The horses were feeding next to the wagon. I was happy to see this and resolved to ask for lodging there, thinking that at least I would be spending the night with Christians. I went up to him and asked, "Who is your passenger?"

"The master is traveling from Kazan to the Crimea," he replied.

While the coachman and I were talking, his master drew apart the curtains inside the carriage. He looked out and, seeing me, said, "I am also spending the night here, but I did not go inside the hut, because Tatar houses are so wretched that I decided to sleep in the carriage." Then, since it was a pleasant evening, he got out to take a walk and we struck up a conversation.

Among my many questions that he responded to, he told me the following about himself.

"Up to the age of sixty-five I served as a high-ranking captain in the navy. As I grew old I developed gout, an incurable infirmity. I retired and went to live in the Crimea on my wife's farm, and I was almost constantly sick. My wife was an extravagant and impulsive woman who loved to play cards. She was bored living with a sick man, so she left me and went to Kazan to live with our daughter, who happened to be married to a civil servant there. She cleaned me out and even took all the servants with her, leaving me only with one eight-year-old boy, my godson.

"I lived alone for about three years. The boy who served me was very capable and took care of all my household chores. He cleaned the room, fired the stove, cooked porridge for me, and heated the samovar. Yet despite all this he was extremely lively and energetic and an impossible mischief-maker. He was incessantly running around, banging, shouting, and carrying on, all of which greatly disturbed me. Because of my illness, and probably from boredom as well, I always loved to read spiritual literature. I had a great book of Saint Gregory Palamas's teaching on the Jesus prayer, which I read from almost continually. At times I would also practice the prayer itself. My boy was a nuisance, and no threats or punishments could keep him from his pranks. So I came up with an idea: I began to make him sit on a footstool next to me and ordered him to repeat continually the Jesus prayer. At first he was not very happy about this and tried everything he could to get out of doing it, or else he would just say nothing at all.

In order to get him to obey, I took to keeping a rod beside me. When he was repeating the prayer, I would quietly read a book or listen to his pronunciation. But as soon as he stopped, I would show him the rod and it would frighten him enough to start the prayer again. This had a very calming effect on me, for it brought quiet to my house. After a short time I noticed that there was no more need of the rod, for the boy was now obeying me more eagerly and willingly. Then I noticed a complete change in his wild character; he became quieter and more reserved and performed his household chores better than before. This made me happy and I started giving him more freedom. Do you know what happened finally? He became so used to the prayer that he repeated it continually, almost all the time, whatever he happened to be doing, and without any urging from me. When I questioned him about it, he replied that he had an irresistible desire to pray unceasingly.

" 'And what do you feel when you pray?' I asked the boy.

" 'Nothing, really—except that it's very nice when I'm praying.'

" 'So—is that good?'

" 'I don't know—what can I say?'

" 'Are you happy?'

" 'Yes, I'm happy.'

"He was already twelve years old when the Crimean War broke out and, taking him with me, I went to stay with my daughter in Kazan. There he lived in the kitchen with the other servants, and he was very bored. He complained to me that the others would play and fool around among themselves, bothering him and making fun of him and preventing him from praying. Finally, after about three months he came to me and said, 'I'm going home. It's unbearably boring and noisy for me here.'

" 'How can you travel so far alone in the winter?' I asked. 'Wait until I'm ready to go, and I'll take you with me.'

"The next day my boy disappeared. We searched everywhere for him, but he was nowhere to be found. At last I received a letter from the Crimea, from some people who had stayed behind on our farm, informing me that on April 4, the day after Easter, the boy had been found dead in my empty house. He was lying on the floor in my room, with his hands devoutly folded on his chest, a cap under his head, and he was wearing the same thin frock coat that he had worn when he lived with me, and was wearing when he left. And so he was buried in my garden. After I received this news I was completely astonished at how the boy had managed to get to the farm so quickly. He left on February 26 and was found on April 4. To cover about two thousand miles in one month—why, even with God's help, you'd still need horses! You would have to travel about sixty-five miles a day—and then, without any warm clothing or a passport or a penny in your pocket. Let's say that maybe somebody gave him a ride along the way, but even that could not have happened without God's specific providence and care for him. Well, now, my boy tasted the fruits of prayer," the master concluded, "while I, at my ripe old age, have not yet attained to the measure of it that he had acquired."

I said to him, "Batyushka, there is a splendid book by the blessed Gregory Palamas, which you used to read. I know that book, but it primarily discusses the oral form of the Jesus prayer. What you should read is a book called the *Philokalia*. There you will find the complete and perfected teaching on how to attain to the spiritual level of the Jesus prayer, in the mind and in the heart, and taste of its sweetest fruits." Then I showed him the *Philokalia* and noticed that he was quite pleased to accept my advice. He promised to obtain a copy of the book for himself.

"My God," I thought to myself, "what wondrous manifestations of God's power are revealed through this prayer and how wise and edifying are such occurrences! A rod had taught the boy to pray and it even served as a means of acquiring consolation! Could it not be that the very grief and sufferings that we encounter on the path of prayer are, in fact, God's own 'rod'? If so, why is it that we are so afraid and distraught when these are sent our way, by the very hand of our Heavenly Father, Who is filled with such boundless love, and when these 'rods' teach us to be more attentive to our prayer and lead us to that inexpressible consolation?"

When I finished relating my stories, I said to my spiritual father, "For God's sake, forgive me—I have talked for too long! The holy Fathers say that even spiritual conversation is vainglory if it is unrestrained. It is now time for me to go and join my fellow traveler to Jersualem. Pray for me, a wretched sinner, that in His infinite mercy the Lord will grant me a good journey."

"My beloved brother in Christ, with all my heart I wish that the grace of God, abounding with love, will bless your journey and go with you, as the angel Raphael went with Tobias!"

GLOSSARY

BASHMAKI. A special shoe worn over walking shoes or boots.

BATYUSHKA. "Little father." At the time the pilgrim writes (the nineteenth century), this term of address was still used as a respectful yet affectionate form of address for one's father or other respected men such as teachers, priests, and nobles. Today it is usually used only when addressing priests.

CHET'-MINEI. A twelve-volume (one for each month) collection of readings from the lives of the saints for every day of the year, arranged in the order in which their feast days occur. It also contains all the books of the Bible along with various other articles on spiritual subjects.

CHOTKI. A rosary or prayer rope: a circular string of knots, usually one hundred but often more or less, used to count the number of Jesus prayers said. Sometimes also used for other prayers as well.

CHURCH SLAVONIC. The language used in the Liturgy of the Russian Orthodox Church. It was devised, along with the Cyrillic alphabet, by the Greek missionaries to the Slavs, Saints Cyril and Methodios, in the ninth century. It remains the liturgical language of the Orthodox Church in Russia and other Slavic countries to this day.

DARK WATER. A popular expression for the disease glaucoma.

FOOL FOR CHRIST (Russian *yurodiviy*). A person who takes on an extreme form of asceticism in which even the appearance of sanity is abandoned and madness is feigned for the sake of Christ. "Holy fools" like this were a fairly common sight in Russia right up until Soviet times and can even sometimes be seen today. The pilgrim was thought to be a fool for Christ by the landowner in the Fourth Narrative because he seemed too well educated to be a simple peasant.

KSENDA. A Polish, and thus probably Roman Catholic, priest.

LAPTI. Coarse linen shoes or sandals worn by peasants.

MATUSHKA. "Little mother." The feminine equivalent of *batyushka*, used similarly in the pilgrim's time as a form of address for women. Today it is used only when addressing a priest's wife or a professed nun.

MIR. The assembly of all the peasant householders in a village. An ancient institution that endowed peasants with a certain degree of self-government, since the landowner was excluded from its membership.

ONOOCHI. Long strips of coarse linen that were wrapped around the feet and legs and worn by Russian peasants instead of stockings.

PHILOKALIA (Greek). "Love of the Beautiful." A collection of mystical and ascetical writings of the Fathers of the Eastern Orthodox Church. In Russian, the book is called *Dobrotolyubie*, "Love of the Good."

PRESANCTIFIED GIFTS. Reserved Holy Communion, kept in a special container on the altar table and taken for distribution to the sick or dying.

SCHIMA MONK/NUN (Russian *skhimnik/skhimnitsa*). A fully ordained monk in Orthodox monasticism, living in strict seclusion.

STARETS (plural *startsi*). "Elder." A monk distinguished for his saintliness, long experience in the spiritual life, and, especially, a unique gift for guiding other souls. Traditionally, the *startsi* were sought out by people for guidance, and entire monastic communities would often grow up around them.

THEOTOKOS (Greek). Birthgiver of God; the Virgin Mary.